# ANATOMY OF
# DECEIT

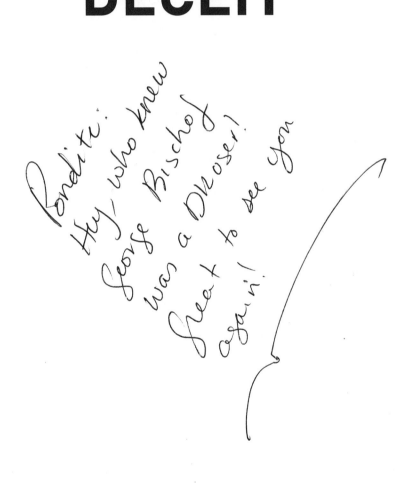

Rondita:
Hey, who knew
George Bischof
was a DKroser!
Great to see you
again!

# ANATOMY OF
# DECEIT

### How the Bush Administration Used the Media
### to Sell the Iraq War and Out a Spy

## MARCY WHEELER

VASTER BOOKS
BERKELEY, CALIFORNIA

Editor: Safir Ahmed
Copy Editor: Evan Camfield
Proofreader: Emily DeHuff
Cover and interior design: Josh Michels


Published by Vaster Books,
an imprint of Vaster Media, Inc.
2625 Alcatraz Avenue #282
Berkeley, CA 94705
www.vasterbooks.com


ISBN10: 0-9791761-0-7
ISBN13: 978-0-9791761-0-4

Printed in the United States of America
on acid-free, recycled paper

Distributed by Publishers Group West

# CONTENTS

# PROLOGUE

People often ask me why I continue to write about the CIA leak case. Why spend the time? I'm an ordinary citizen. I live in Michigan and work as a self-employed business consultant, developing corporate training programs. I worry about keeping clients happy and meeting their deadlines and paying my bills. My friends knew I blogged, under the name "emptywheel," at The Next Hurrah. But they didn't understand how I got wrapped up in the Valerie Plame story, why I was forgoing billable hours and sleep to follow every twist and turn of the case.

It all started with an argument I got into with one of my blogmates, Meteor Blades. It was July 2005, and *New York Times* journalist Judith Miller was preparing to go to jail rather than reveal her source in the CIA leak case. Most of the media saw her decision as a heroic stand against an unjust infringement of a reporter's privilege. In response to such coverage, I asked a hypothetical question about whether, as they become more and more solicitous of administration plans, journalists lose their claim to First Amendment privileges. After all, no one would defend the right of an Enron public relations flack to hide the criminal behavior of its CEO in the name of the First Amendment. As reporters like Miller uncritically repeated the stories pitched by the administration, were they acting in a PR role, rather than as journalists?

Meteor Blades worked for many years as a journalist, serving as the editorials and op-ed editor for two major newspapers. He defended Miller's right to First Amendment protection fiercely, arguing that the reporter's privilege must be defended for all journalists, because even leaks from politically driven sources contribute to government transparency.

Arguing with Meteor Blades is a daunting proposition. He is one of the wise men of the blogosphere, with a life experience and perspective far exceeding my own. So to defend my argument, I wrote a series of posts reexamining Miller's reporting from Iraq. I had a hunch that the happy stories she told about the WMD hunt in Iraq and administration efforts to silence a critic, Joe Wilson, were all part of a unified strategy to sustain their shared WMD claims. There was a real continuity of tactics between Miller's activities in Iraq and her involvement in the CIA leak case.

My argument was either persuasive or prescient, because by the time the full extent of Miller's involvement was revealed in November 2005, Meteor Blades had conceded I was right.

My investigation into Miller's reporting was the beginning of a year-plus attempt to understand what had happened in the CIA leak case. As I finished my series on Miller's reporting, I started tracking a story—obviously leaked—about a memo summarizing the State Department's judgment of allegations that Iraq attempted to buy uranium from Niger. From that point forward, I was hooked, and I was following the related developments on a near-daily basis.

It was this kind of sustained attention that has led bloggers to a lot of key scoops in this case. The most impressive is eRiposte's discovery that someone laundered the content of the Niger forgeries before cabling that content to the CIA. Joshua Micah Marshall demonstrated that contrary to columnist Robert Novak's claims, when Novak used the word "operative" to refer to a CIA employee, he usually meant a clandestine officer. Jane Hamsher was the first to reveal that *Time* magazine's Viveca Novak told Karl Rove's lawyer that her colleague, Matt Cooper, considered Rove his source. With other bloggers, I discovered—six months before it was "scooped" in the mainstream press—that Richard Armitage was Robert

Novak's unknown source. In February 2006, I reported (ten days before the traditional media) that George Bush and Dick Cheney authorized Scooter Libby to leak classified documents to journalists. In May 2006, I showed that Libby's stories about Cheney's involvement in the leak case made no sense, which meant Cheney was probably more intimately involved than Libby let on. Jeralyn Merritt used her background as a defense attorney to get clarifications from Rove's lawyer about Rove's nonindictment.

But that's not the most important role bloggers played in this story—most (though by no means all) of the "scoops" we found were eventually covered by traditional journalists. Rather, bloggers brought persistence and perspective to this story. With each new revelation, we questioned and reassessed the dominant narrative about the case. As a result, we often saw through the contradictions and the spin that many traditional journalists regurgitated unquestioningly.

The CIA leak case is a story of how our elected leaders exploited the weaknesses of our media, first to deceive us into war and then to bully those who tried to do what the press should have done: call our leaders on their deceptions. Which is why I found it all so irresistible—it's a story that goes to the heart of our ability to sustain our democracy. It questions whether we, as a society, have lost our ability to exercise oversight over our government and whether we can prevent it from pursuing catastrophic policies against the will of most of the citizenry.

This is an ongoing story, so I can only guess how it might end. But whether or not the special prosecutor in the case, Patrick Fitzgerald, wins a conviction of Scooter Libby, I want others to know the real story hiding behind the flaccid conventional wisdom. If we're going to reclaim the consent of the governed, we are going to have to reclaim the storytelling function, because the media has largely lost its ability to tell stories with the distance or wisdom needed to serve the truth.

But the real reason I dedicated so much time to this story is that I believe it matters. I said I'm an ordinary citizen, but I do bring a particular perspective to the story. For a Ph.D. at the University of Michigan, I studied a literary-journalistic form called the feuilleton, a kind of conversational essay that appears in a newspaper in its own section. Feuilletons first appeared in response to Napoleonic censorship, and in the two hundred years since, they have often become important at moments when political polarization or government censorship has degraded traditional news reporting into nothing more than the parroting of ideological talking points. At such times, the feuilleton has served as a place where writers, using ordinary language, could tell of important events in a more meaningful way.

In Communist Czechoslovakia in the 1970s, a group of citizens started writing feuilletons, telling an unofficial version of events. They shared them among friends, copying them over and passing them on in a form of self-publishing. These citizens would go on to lead a revolution, the peaceful Velvet Revolution. One of these citizens would even become president.

You see, I came to this story knowing the power of ordinary citizens speaking the truth.

CHAPTER 1

# SIXTEEN WORDS

(September 2002–March 2003)

---

*Saddam has perfected the game of cheat and retreat, and is very skilled in the art of denial and deception.* — Dick Cheney, speaking to the Veterans of Foreign Wars, August 28, 2002

On January 28, 2003, when the sergeant at arms of the U.S. House of Representatives declared, "Mr. Speaker, the President of the United States," George W. Bush started slowly making his way through the chamber, shaking hands with those crowding the aisle, while Vice President Dick Cheney stood on the dais, quietly monitoring the proceedings. When Bush reached the dais, he turned to the two men—Cheney and Speaker of the House Dennis Hastert—standing above and behind him, and handed each a copy of the State of the Union speech he was about to deliver. Hastert put his copy to the side, almost carelessly. Cheney placed his directly in front of his seat, his fingers tapping it with satisfaction.

On this occasion, President Bush handed a speech to Cheney that the vice president had created. The most important part of the speech, after all, would make the case to the American people for a preemptive invasion of Iraq. For more than two years—arguably as many as five—Cheney and his allies had been manufacturing a case for this war. The vice president had set up his own shadow National Security Council—a network of neoconservative loyalists, placed throughout the administration to support the vice president's hawkish foreign policy. In the case of Iraq, Cheney's allies reviewed raw intelligence, looking for evidence of weapons of mass destruction (WMDs), even if it had been dismissed by the intelligence agencies as not credible.

Beyond that, Cheney had close allies in the Iraqi exile community who provided defectors telling stories of the grave danger that Saddam posed to the world. Cheney and his chief of staff, I. Lewis "Scooter" Libby, Jr., exerted unusual pressure on the intelligence agencies, making repeated—and unprecedented—visits to the CIA.[1] As the vice president's trusted and competent confidant, Libby managed bureaucratic infighting to ensure that information flowed directly to Cheney, who sometimes kept things from others, even the president.[2] Cheney and his allies would not wait for—or even trust—the traditional intelligence channels to assess or develop the case for war. Instead, they built that case themselves.

And tonight was the night to close the deal—Bush would deliver the speech to persuade the American people that the cause was just.

In reality, the White House had made the decision to go to war at least ten months earlier; Cheney had told a group of Republican senators in March 2002 that the question was not whether the United States would invade Iraq but when it would do so.[3] By September, the administration had launched a prowar campaign directed primarily at Congress and the United Nations. On October 1, under pressure from Democrats, the administration produced a national intelligence estimate (NIE) in record time—three weeks—preventing analysts from thoroughly debating the document's judgments.[4] Three days later, a declassified version, stripped of most of the dissents, was released.[5] With midterm elections a month away, selling the war to Congress didn't prove too difficult. The administration rushed through the Iraq War resolution, which was approved by the House on October 10 and the Senate the next day. This was followed by a relentless drumbeat of accusations and allegations about Iraq's pursuit of deadly weapons and the imminent danger it posed to the free world.

And now it was time to sell the Iraq War to the American public. With the eyes of the nation focused on him, President Bush began reading his speech. His performance was choreographed to make him look stern, tough, and resolute. In delivering the speech, Bush rarely smiled, and he frequently pursed his lips or furrowed and raised his eyebrows. He delivered the words that had been so carefully crafted by others in his administration for maximum effect.

About forty-five minutes into the speech, he made the three claims that formed the core of the case for war against Iraq:

> From three Iraqi defectors we know that Iraq, in the late 1990s, had several mobile biological weapons labs. These are designed to produce germ warfare agents, and can be moved from place to a place to evade inspectors. Saddam Hussein has not disclosed these facilities. He's given no evidence that he has destroyed them.
>
> The International Atomic Energy Agency confirmed in the 1990s that Saddam Hussein had an advanced nuclear weapons development program, had a design for a nuclear weapon and was working on five different methods of enriching uranium for a bomb. The British government has learned that Saddam Hussein recently sought significant quantities of uranium from Africa. Our intelligence sources tell us that he has attempted to purchase high-strength aluminum tubes suitable for nuclear weapons production. Saddam Hussein has not credibly explained these activities. He clearly has much to hide.[6]

Bush proceeded to tell America that the nation would accept no compromise. He promised that if Saddam didn't disarm, the United States would go to war. He assured the nation that God was on our side: "The liberty we prize is not America's gift to the world, it is God's gift to humanity.... We do not claim to know all the ways of Providence, yet we can trust in them, placing our confidence in the loving God behind all of life, and all of history."

Bush's claims about WMDs were thin—relying on what conservative pundits might call Clintonesque word games.[7] Rather than asserting that Saddam had mobile bioweapons labs (MBLs) in 2003, Bush said only that three defectors claimed he had them in the late 1990s. Rather than state that Saddam had acquired enriched uranium from Niger, Bush claimed only that the British government had learned Saddam had "sought" the material. Rather than claim that Saddam wanted aluminum tubes to produce nuclear weapons, Bush said only that the tubes were "suitable" for nuclear weapons production. Bush implied, without really saying so, that all three claims meant Iraq still had WMDs. That's because the administration had been warned—by its own intelligence community—not to use those claims.

While the most discussed part of Bush's speech regarding Iraq would later turn out to be the "sixteen words" ("The British government has learned that Saddam Hussein recently sought significant quantities of uranium from Africa"), the administration had in fact been warned against using all three of the claims Bush made.

A week later, on February 5, 2003, Secretary of State Colin Powell would stand before the UN Security Council and make two of the same claims. Unlike Bush, Powell did not state that Saddam had sought uranium from Niger—he later explained that the claim was not standing the test of time. But Powell elaborated on the mobile bioweapons lab assertion, saying the labs could produce huge amounts of biological materials—each trailer producing as much as the Iraqis had before the Gulf War. Powell described an accident in which twelve workers purportedly died from exposure to biological weapons. And he offered an extended argument that the aluminum tubes were intended for centrifuges. He admitted there was controversy about the tubes, but neglected to mention that the "other experts" he lumped in with the Iraqis as dissenters were the best experts on centrifuges in the United States. Through the entire speech, Powell kept hammering on the quality of the evidence for his claims: "Every statement I make today is backed up by sources, solid sources. These are not assertions. What we're giving you are facts and conclusions based on solid intelligence."

Only they weren't based on solid intelligence. And like the president, those writing Powell's speech had been warned.[8]

* * *

It's worth reviewing the nature of the intelligence claims and the means by which those claims were championed. The story turns out to be not just one of contested claims of intelligence but one of outright deceit.

The assertion that the Iraqis had moved their biological weapons labs onto trailers to evade detection seems to be the handiwork of a colorful and shady character named Ahmed Chalabi.

As the leader of the Iraqi National Congress (INC), an opposition group created in 1992 with the support of the CIA, Chalabi spent the early 1990s fomenting an overthrow of Saddam Hussein. The INC produced anti-Saddam propaganda and eventually shared the stories of defectors with the CIA. By 1996, after two failed coup attempts had soured the CIA on direct overthrow (and on Chalabi himself), he began to seek allies among the hardliners who were pushing the Clinton administration to adopt a more confrontational policy against Iraq. And in 1998, when the United Nations Special Commission (UNSCOM) inspections in Iraq had reached an impasse, the agency's deputy executive chairman, Charles Duelfer, seized on Chalabi's promise to provide new intelligence. Duelfer ordered the weapons inspector Scott Ritter to meet with Chalabi to see what he had to offer.

Ritter didn't learn much from Chalabi. But Chalabi seems to have learned quite a bit from Ritter, as Ritter recounted later in his book:

> I was under pressure from Charles Duelfer to make this new relationship work, and I proceeded to brief Chalabi on UNSCOM's understanding about what Iraq might be hiding. This included speculation about the possible existence of mobile biological laboratories and agent production facilities.... When, several years after leaving UNSCOM, I was to read through the intelligence provided by Chalabi's "source" ("Curveball"), which formed the centerpiece of the Bush administration's case for war, I was struck by just how similar this data was to some of the speculative "intelligence gaps" I had provided to Ahmed Chalabi back in 1998.[9]

In 1999, a year after Chalabi's meetings with Scott Ritter, Iraqi defectors telling stories of MBLs started showing up.

The first of these defectors was the brother of Chalabi's bodyguard, who showed up in Germany as an exile escaping an embezzlement charge in Iraq. Later code-named Curveball, he sought asylum in Germany, claiming to have helped build MBLs before he left Iraq. He provided sketches of the trailers he said he had designed. He named co-workers. But once he received asylum, he stopped cooperating. The Germans warned the Americans he might be a fabricator and mentally unstable. And key CIA officials, including the Berlin station chief and the head of operations in Europe, expressed doubt about Curveball's stories.

The intelligence community said three other defectors corroborated Curveball's story, even though it found none of them credible. One defector's story was largely discounted when he told it in 2001.[10] Another appears to have failed a lie detector test.[11] And the CIA determined the last, a major in Iraq's intelligence service, to be a fabricator coached by the INC eight months before the State of the Union speech. That same month, the major appeared as an anonymous source in a *Vanity Fair* article, saying he bought eight Renault trucks and converted them to MBLs. "They look like meat cars, yogurt cars," he told the magazine. "And inside is a laboratory, with incubators for bacteria, microscopes, air-conditioning."[12] The story cites Duelfer, the deputy chair of UNSCOM, saying the defector's tales were consistent with what UNSCOM inspections found. When the NIE of October 2002 cited the major as someone who corroborated Curveball's story, they sourced it to the *Vanity Fair* article.[13] That was the quality of the "corroboration" for Curveball's story: anonymous quotes in a magazine article.

When, in June 2003, the administration claimed—despite evidence to the contrary—that trailers it found in Iraq were MBLs, Chalabi took credit: "The only tangible things they have found are the mobile labs, which our defectors talked about."[14] Chalabi's allies were all fabricators, but their stories about an active Iraqi bioweapons program resonated well inside an administration eager to hear it.

The claim that Saddam had sought (or bought) yellowcake uranium from Niger also had murky origins, in this case involving burglaries, forgeries, and Italian spies. In February 2000, Antonio Nucera, a colonel in SISMI, the Italian intelligence agency, offered to introduce a longtime agency source to a down-on-his-luck former colleague as a favor. The source, La Signora, who worked at the Nigerien embassy in Rome, had sold codebooks and documents from the embassy to SISMI in the past. Nucera thought La Signora might be able to provide similar materials to his former colleague,

Rocco Martino, which Martino could then sell to make some money.

Then several curious events took place. The Nigerien embassy was bur-glarized and some stamps and letterhead were taken. Later, La Signora provided embassy seals and correspondence to Martino. Then someone—it's not clear who—took those materials and crafted really sloppy forgeries of documents alleging a uranium deal between Niger and Iraq.[15] By early 2001, rumors began circulating that Niger had sold uranium to Iraq. They took on weight when SISMI shared news of a uranium deal with intelli-gence services in Europe and the United States. Around the same time, Martino showed up at European intelligence agencies trying to sell copies of documents purporting to reveal the uranium deal.

The forgeries had blatant inaccuracies relating to names and titles of officials, but before the information from the forgeries was cabled to the CIA, someone fixed the mistakes to make the intelligence more believ-able.[16] And as to the contract for the alleged agreement between Niger and Iraq? It may never have existed, except as a "summary" cable from SISMI providing the details of the contract.[17] Someone again doctored content from the forged documents to make them more useful as a prop to justify war. In a way, the Nigerien claim was forged twice—once in the creation of the documents, and the second time in the correction of those documents to make them more plausible to intelligence services.

Eventually, the forged documents would form the basis for at least seven intelligence reports shared by agencies around the world. Some in the intelligence community raised commonsense refutations of the allegations. How could Niger send twenty-five ten-ton trucks across the Sahara unno-ticed?[18] Why would Iraq try to buy yellowcake uranium when it already had 550 tons of it?[19] Others remained skeptical that the United States could ever disprove the claims. Why would the Nigeriens admit to selling uranium to Iraq if we asked them?[20]

Yet one thing made the uranium claims more believable. The SISMI cables claimed that Iraq began negotiating the deal when Wissam al-Zahawie, the Iraqi ambassador to the Vatican, visited Niger in 1999. But on the same trip, Zahawie also traveled to three other African nations—Benin, Burkina

Faso, and Congo-Brazzaville—trying to persuade African heads of state to visit Iraq in hopes of chipping away at the sanctions regime the United States set up after the Gulf War. Zahawie's visit had nothing to do with a uranium deal.[21] But by playing off an event that was known to have taken place—Zahawie's trip—the forgers made the uranium claim more plausible. Even the British fell for it, issuing a white paper in September 2002 reporting that Iraq had tried to buy uranium from Niger.

In the end, the United States made four inquiries to check out the claims, and the French (who oversee the consortium that handles Niger's uranium) made at least two. All came back negative. By fall 2002, the CIA was convinced the Niger allegations were wrong.

On October 5, 2002, the White House submitted to the CIA a draft of a speech President Bush was to deliver in Cincinnati two days later that contained the sentence, "The [Iraqi] regime has been caught attempting to purchase up to 500 metric tons of uranium oxide from Africa." The CIA's response memo, which outlined all the details that needed to be changed in the speech, advised the White House to remove the sentence. The next draft, however, still had the claim. This time, CIA director George Tenet personally called Stephen Hadley, Bush's deputy national security advisor, and told him: "The President should not be a fact witness on this issue."[22] A more colorful version of Tenet's message to Hadley comes via Bob Woodward's book *State of Denial:* "You need to take this fucking sentence out because we don't believe it."[23] In any case, the CIA reiterated that warning in a fax, listing three reasons not to use the claim, addressed to both Hadley and Michael Gerson, the speechwriter.[24] When Bush delivered the speech on October 7, the sentence was not in it.

But the Niger uranium claim didn't die. Just days later, an Italian journalist, Elisabetta Burba, brought a copy of the forgeries to the United States embassy in Rome for vetting. The CIA did not accept the forgeries, perhaps because the CIA had already dismissed the Niger allegations. Instead, the embassy sent them through the State Department's Bureau on Nonproliferation, which reported to Undersecretary of State John Bolton, a close ally of Cheney.[25] Before long, the Niger uranium claim was back in circulation among the administration. Bolton's office included it in a December 19 fact sheet on Iraq's declaration to UN weapons inspectors.

The White House received one more warning not to use the Niger claim—it came in the form of a memo from the top intelligence officer on Africa to Bush's security aides days before the State of the Union speech. The memo said the Niger claim was baseless and should be laid to rest.[26] Yet the warning wasn't heeded, and the claim ended up in Bush's speech to the nation anyway. Repetition of the unsubstantiated intelligence won out over vetting and verification.

The third key claim in Bush's speech, that Iraq was trying to buy aluminum tubes for nuclear weapons production, first surfaced in the President's Daily Briefing in April 2001. Iraq was attempting to acquire sixty thousand high-strength aluminum tubes, which the CIA said had "little use other than for a uranium enrichment program," even while admitting using such tubes "would be inefficient."[27] The argument was that Iraq would use the tubes to construct a centrifuge. By spinning uranium in tubes at very high speeds, you can separate heavier from lighter uranium to make it weapons grade uranium. In 1991, the Iraqis had indeed used centrifuges to enrich uranium.

The assertion that Iraq wanted the tubes for use in centrifuges was aggressively pushed by a CIA analyst named Joe Turner.[28] A mechanical engineer, Turner had expertise working with the United States' own centrifuges. But his efforts to champion the centrifuge theory had as much to do with controlling information as they did with expertise.

Turner consistently prevented others from assessing his argument. He engaged another contractor to review his work, but he didn't give this contractor the specifications of the rockets Iraq used, so the contractor was unable to adequately consider the conventional weapon explanation.[29] Turner also ignored the United States military's own rocket specialists, who recommended he talk to the Italians, since their Medusa rockets matched the dimensions of the aluminum tubes.[30]

Turner misrepresented things to sustain his argument. In one case, he claimed the specs for the centrifuge he suggested Iraq was building were closer to those of the tubes than they really were.[31] According to David Albright, a nonproliferation expert, after Turner made a presentation to the International Atomic Energy Agency (IAEA) in July 2001, he reported back to the CIA that the IAEA agreed with his arguments, when in fact the agency considered his analysis "really bad."[32] Nevertheless, at least nine reports based on Turner's analysis made their way to top administration officials between July 2001 and July 2002.[33]

Ignored completely was the analysis of the U.S. Department of Energy (DOE) and the IAEA, the top experts on the kind of centrifuges Iraq had used to enrich uranium. On April 11, 2001, one day after top administration officials saw the CIA report based on Turner's assessment, the DOE offered its own initial analysis: The tubes could be used for uranium enrichment, the agency said, but the specifications would make their use very inefficient, partly because the tubes were the wrong size to work effectively. And since Iraq wasn't known to be seeking all the other parts that would be needed to construct a centrifuge, the tubes probably weren't for centrifuges. By May 2001, the DOE reported that Iraq had used very similar tubes in the past as casings for conventional rockets. In July 2001, the IAEA seconded the DOE conclusion, noting that Iraq had used tubes like these in a program going back to 1989 and had declared the rockets to UNSCOM in 1996. The DOE and IAEA had data and expertise on their side, but Turner's explanations of the aluminum tubes provided a sense of urgency for the prowar campaign, which the administration officially launched in September 2002. As with the intelligence on the MBLs and the Niger allegations, the administration placed more weight on the intelligence that supported its case for war.

After Bush's State of the Union speech in January 2003 and before the Iraq invasion began, the administration would receive hard evidence that all three claims were false. On February 9, 2003, weapons inspectors from the United Nations Monitoring, Verification and Inspections Commission (UNMOVIC) visited the building in which Curveball claimed Saddam had manufactured MBLs. The building did not fit Curveball's description and could not have been used as Curveball described because the walls would prevent the trailers from moving in and out of the building. On March 3, 2003, after conducting extensive research, the IAEA validated Iraqi claims that the aluminum tubes were for conventional rockets and provided detailed explanations for all the suspicions raised about the tubes. And on March 7, the IAEA confirmed what a State Department analyst had observed back in mid-October: The documents describing an Iraqi uranium purchase from Niger were crude, embarrassing forgeries.

And so, twelve days before the war started, all three primary WMD claims that Bush used to justify the war had been proven false.

\* \* \*

One other group of U.S. experts looked into the overall allegation that Iraq was developing WMDs. It was called the Joint Iraq Task Force (JITF) and was convened under the aegis of the CIA in September 2001. At the time, the CIA had few sources in Iraq, since it had ended most of its programs when the United States had withdrawn weapons inspectors in 1998. The JITF focused on developing sources inside Iraq who could provide intelligence about any efforts to make WMDs.

The JITF contacted exiled Iraqi scientists as well as Iraqis living in the United States, Europe, and Asia whose family members were scientists remaining in Iraq. JITF officials figured the family members might be able to establish contact with the scientists involved in any reactivated WMD program in Iraq. But all the family members reported the same news— Iraq didn't have any active WMD programs. The JITF also vetted "walk-ins," the Iraqi exiles—including INC defectors—peddling stories about WMDs to Western intelligence agencies. The group determined many of those defectors were obvious fabricators.[34] Yet the JITF was seen as offering no evidence of WMDs in Iraq.[35] The program was deemed a failure and terminated.[36]

In his speech, Bush ignored the evidence the JITF had gathered showing that there were no WMDs.[37] But his administration didn't ignore everything about the task force. Among its members was a CIA operative named Valerie Plame Wilson.[38] Within a few months, the administration would pay quite a bit of attention to her.

\* \* \*

Bush dismissed any evidence that ran contrary to his claims by insisting that Saddam was deceiving the international community. Cheney would echo that, asserting that Saddam Hussein was adept at denying access to his WMD programs and deceiving weapons inspectors. "Saddam Hussein is continuing his decade-old game of defiance, delay and deception," Cheney told the Conservative Political Action Committee two days after Bush's speech. Cheney listed the inventories of chemical and biological weapons Iraq was purported to have, though he did not mention any of the three claims that Bush had made in his speech. But Cheney also signaled his approval of Bush's performance, which Cheney himself had helped craft. "Two nights ago, I was very proud as the President delivered his State of the Union address and set forth a full agenda for the nation for 2003 and beyond," Cheney said. "This is going to be a consequential year in the history of our nation and in the history of freedom."[39]

The aerial bombardment of Baghdad began on March 19, 2003.

# CHAPTER 2

# DECONSTRUCTING JUDY

(March–July 2003)

---

*My job isn't to assess the government's information and be an independent intelligence analyst myself. My job is to tell readers of* **The New York Times** *what the government thought about Iraq's arsenal.* — Judith Miller, quoted in Michael Massing's "Now They Tell Us," *The New York Review of Books,* February 26, 2004

The story in *The New York Times* offered a stark warning about Iraq:

> State Department and intelligence officials said today they believed that Iraq had acquired enough enriched uranium and sensitive technology to make one nuclear weapon by the end of this year.... This conclusion, intelligence officials said, is based on Iraq's ambitious nuclear program, which they described as far exceeding either the Iraqis' power requirements or programs aimed at commercial use.[40]

Anonymous administration sources claiming that Iraq had the technology and the uranium and might soon have a nuclear bomb—it was precisely the kind of warning we heard throughout 2002, leading up to the Iraq war in 2003. Only this warning came much earlier. The *Times* story was published on June 9, 1981, after the Israelis had bombed Iraq's Osirak nuclear reactor in a preemptive attack they said would prevent Iraq from using the reactor to enrich uranium. The article suggested Iraq remained a proliferation threat, which validated the Israeli attack.

The story, written by Judith Miller, exemplified what have since become hallmarks of her journalistic career: unnamed highly placed sources pushing a hawkish message. Her stories fit the same pattern in the months preceding the Iraq invasion in 2003.

Miller entered the field of journalism in the 1970s, in the wake of the Watergate scandal, when Bob Woodward and Carl Bernstein at *The Washington Post* had set a new standard for investigative journalism. In a field dominated by men, Miller thrived by working long hours and by forming close connections with insiders, people like Ronald Reagan's assistant secretary of state, Richard Burt, and assistant secretary of defense, Richard Perle. In 1983, she became the *Times's* first female Cairo bureau chief, covering much of the Middle East. Later, she served as the deputy bureau chief in Washington.

Her many years of working on security issues in the Middle East allowed Miller to develop relationships with Middle Eastern leaders as well as domestic experts on terrorism like Richard Clarke and top administration officials like Douglas Feith and John Bolton. Drawing on those relationships, Miller's stories featured an army of anonymous "senior administration officials" who would give her exclusive scoops by leaking information. And she was an aggressive, hardworking journalist, pursuing stories about national security relentlessly. She traveled to Taliban-controlled Afghanistan to research Al Qaeda. She witnessed a public hanging in Sudan.[41] She watched the Israeli interrogation of an alleged Hamas funder.[42]

At its best, Miller's work provided warnings of real dangers, as with her reporting on Osama bin Laden starting in 1996, and the Pulitzer Prize–winning three-part series on Al Qaeda in January 2001, which she co-wrote with colleagues at the *Times*. In July 2001, one of Miller's sources within the administration provided her with an exclusive tip about an intercepted conversation between two Al Qaeda operatives, in which one promised something "so big now that the United States will have to respond."[43] Miller couldn't flesh out the tip well enough to write a story. In any case, when Al Qaeda struck the United States on 9/11, Miller seemed to be one of few public voices that had sounded an alarm.

But her strengths had their ugly flip side—which would eventually completely discredit Miller and lead to her departure from the *Times*. Inside the newsroom, Miller had stepped on a lot of toes over the years— trespassing on other reporters' stories, bypassing supervising editors' decisions—and her aggressiveness often seemed more like bitchiness. For much of her career, a close friendship with the current publisher of the *Times*, Arthur Ochs Sulzberger, Jr., enabled her to get away with this behavior. During Howell Raines's tenure as executive editor, from 2001 to 2003, Miller was treated as a favorite whose stories got published regardless of her journalistic lapses or unprofessional behavior.[44]

Miller's access to powerful sources turned into a too-close affiliation with their goals and a credulity about their claims. The more she published articles pleasing to hawks in the administration, the more they came to her with exclusive stories. Finally, in the lead-up to the Iraq war, her access to scoops turned her into a virtual mouthpiece for the powerful prowar factions in the administration.

Miller had served the Bush administration's purposes well leading up to the war. As early as 1998, she had co-authored a profile of Iraqi exile Khidir Hamza, who described Saddam resorting to torture and killings to speed his nuclear program. In December 2001, she published the dire warnings of another Iraqi defector, Adnan Ihsan Saeed al-Haideri, who alleged that Saddam had recently renewed his interest in acquiring nuclear weapons.

And on September 8, 2002, she partnered with Michael Gordon on a blockbuster article outlining the administration's case for war. The timing of that article was almost as significant as its content. For the hawks in the administration, it was a godsend.

Less than two weeks earlier, Vice President Dick Cheney had given a provocative speech at the national convention of Veterans of Foreign Wars (VFW) in San Antonio—a speech not vetted by the CIA, presenting a policy not approved by Bush—dismissing the efficacy of weapons inspectors in Iraq:[45]

A return of inspectors would provide no assurance whatsoever of his compliance with UN resolutions. On the contrary, there is a great danger that it would provide false comfort that Saddam was somehow "back in his box."[46]

In the same speech, Cheney raised the specter of Iraq's WMDs in stronger terms than used before:

The Iraqi regime has in fact been very busy enhancing its capabilities in the field of chemical and biological agents. And they continue to pursue the nuclear program they began so many years ago.

Cheney's speech forced those espousing a policy of negotiation with Iraq through the United Nations—particularly Secretary of State Colin Powell—on the defensive. And it framed the stakes the administration would use to sell the war to Congress. This was a war about nuclear weapons because Dick Cheney made it a war about nuclear weapons.

At about the same time that Cheney made his incendiary speech, Bush's chief of staff, Andrew H. Card, Jr., convened the White House Iraq Group (WHIG), which would take the lead in marketing the war. A secretive and powerful team, WHIG included presidential advisor Karl Rove, Cheney's chief of staff, Scooter Libby, National Security Advisor Condoleezza Rice, Deputy National Security Advisor Stephen Hadley, communications strategists Karen Hughes and Mary Matalin, speechwriter Michael Gerson, legislative affairs assistant Nicholas Calio, and communications staffer Jim Wilkinson. One of WHIG's initial efforts, a September 4 congressional briefing by Secretary of Defense Donald Rumsfeld, was a complete failure, with senators coming out of the briefing asking what was new and urgent that required the authorization for the use of force. But on September 6, Card announced the launching of a public campaign for the Iraq war, as if it were some kind of new consumer product. He told the *Times:* "From a marketing point of view, you don't introduce new products in August."[47]

Two days later, on September 8, Miller and Gordon played a key role in that prowar campaign with their front-page story in the Sunday *Times*. The article described Iraq's attempts to acquire aluminum tubes—destined to be used to build centrifuges, which would, in turn, enrich uranium, it said. The article reviewed the history of Iraq's nuclear weapons ambitions and described the inventories of nonconventional weapons and missiles unaccounted for since the United Nations Special Commission (UNSCOM) weapons inspections of the 1990s. And in true Miller fashion, the article quoted three Iraqi defectors, all telling of Saddam's plans to build and use WMDs.

At a time when the administration had not yet agreed to complete a National Intelligence Estimate, the consensus document on which policy decisions were normally made, on Iraq, the *Times* article effectively served in its stead. It was the first public, comprehensive case for war. And it had the advantage of appearing, unvetted by intelligence services, on the front page of the nation's most influential newspaper.

But it did more than lay out the case for war—it also set up a blitz of TV appearances that same day by Cheney, Powell, Rice, and Rumsfeld, all echoing the points presented by Miller and Gordon in their article. It also introduced the key metaphors the administration would use throughout its discussions of WMDs: the smoking gun and the mushroom cloud. These images are usually attributed to Rice in her appearance on CNN that day, in which she listed a lot of circumstantial evidence that Saddam had resumed his nuclear program, then warned:

> The problem here is that there will always be some uncertainty about how quickly he can acquire nuclear weapons. But we don't want the smoking gun to be a mushroom cloud.

Rumsfeld, too, would use the metaphors that day. But the metaphors first appeared that morning, in the *Times* article. On the grounds that analysts had underestimated Saddam's nuclear arsenal in the past, the article explained, hardliners "argue that Washington dare not wait until analysts have found hard evidence that Mr. Hussein has acquired a nuclear weapon. The first sign of a 'smoking gun,' they argue, may be a mushroom cloud."

The article served the administration's purposes in another way. Relying on a number of anonymous sources—"hardliners," "senior administration officials," defectors—it reported on highly classified information relating to the aluminum tubes. These anonymous leaks allowed the administration—with the invaluable assistance of Miller and Gordon—to introduce this information into the public debate without having to declassify it, or to reveal the arguments of dissenting voices within the intelligence community. This allowed the top officials to refer back to it, effectively using the reporters as cutouts for the dissemination of classified information. When he appeared on NBC's *Meet the Press,* for example, Cheney feigned caution in speaking about the tubes, then conceded it was okay to do so since the *Times* had made it public:

> There's a story in *The New York Times* this morning—this is—I don't— and I want to attribute the *Times.* I don't want to talk about, obviously, specific intelligence sources, but it's now public that, in fact, [Saddam Hussein] has been seeking to acquire, and we have been able to intercept and prevent him from acquiring through this particular channel, the kinds of tubes that are necessary to build a centrifuge.

The campaign worked. With WHIG's effort, the 9/11 anniversary, and the hefty assist from Miller and the *Times,* not to mention the impending midterm elections, the U.S. House and Senate approved a resolution to authorize the Iraq War and President Bush signed it into law on October 16, 2002.

* * *

Given that WMDs were the primary justification for the war, expectations were high that the United States would find such weapons in Iraq after the invasion. Yet, throughout late 2002, the administration and military planners did almost nothing to prepare for the post-invasion WMD hunt. They had a list of almost a thousand suspected sites, but for many of these sites, the intelligence dated to before the UNSCOM inspectors had withdrawn in 1998. In December 2002, the Army major general in charge of intelligence for the invasion, James A. "Spider" Marks, demanded that he get a dedicated unit to conduct the WMD hunt. What he got was an artillery brigade, newly dubbed the 75th Expedition Task Force (XTF), which had neither the manpower nor the expertise nor the equipment to carry out its task. Ten days before the start of the war the unit received orders — straight from Rumsfeld — that Judith Miller would embed as the sole journalist with the unit.[48] Miller came to dominate the effort, at least for Mobile Exploitation Team (MET) Alpha, a subunit of the XTF with which she traveled. Placing Miller with the XTF appears to have been a key strategy for the WMD hunt. The Pentagon paid much closer attention to who they put in charge of telling the stories about the WMD hunt than they did to the military unit that actually did the hunting.

The plan for the WMD hunt was simple enough: The XTF would travel to the hundreds of suspected weapons sites on the administration's list and perform initial technical analysis. Miller and her unit tried to follow that plan. After the invasion the search began, and Miller dutifully reported the efforts. She described fruitless searches in Najaf, Talil, and Karbala, all suspected weapons sites. She described the excitement of a suspicious substance, only to admit a few days later that the substance had tested negative. By the first week of April, observers had begun to express doubts. Where were the WMDs?

A month after the invasion, those doubts grew more intense. And that's when the strategy of telling good stories about WMDs took priority over actually looking for them. On April 21, Miller published a story that explained away the absence of the WMDs:

> A scientist who claims to have worked in Iraq's chemical weapons program for more than a decade has told an American military team that Iraq destroyed chemical weapons and biological warfare equipment only days before the war began, members of the team said.

> They said the scientist led Americans to a supply of material that
> proved to be the building blocks of illegal weapons, which he claimed
> to have buried as evidence of Iraq's illicit weapons programs.

In this and an April 24 article, Miller described the scientist bringing the
MET Alpha unit to a site where, the scientist said, he had buried chemical
precursors to chemical weapons, and to a laboratory full of broken equipment in a warehouse complex. He described the testing of "unconventional
agents" on dogs within the previous year. And in the days before the war,
he explained, Iraq had burned chemical and biological equipment and a
warehouse that housed a research facility.

The scientist also told the Americans that Iraq was cooperating with Al
Qaeda, the story said. Miller's story seemed to validate all the key administration justifications for the war:

> The officials' account of the scientist's assertions and the discovery of
> the buried material, which they described as the most important dis-
> covery to date in the hunt for illegal weapons, supports the Bush
> administration's charges that Iraq continued to develop those weapons
> and lied to the United Nations about it. Finding and destroying illegal
> weapons was a major justification for the war.
>
> The officials' accounts also provided an explanation for why
> United States forces had not yet turned up banned weapons in Iraq. The
> failure to find such weapons has become a political issue in Washington.

The scientist appeared to answer all of the administration's prayers. But
it turned out that he was too good to be true.

First, Miller claimed not to have spoken to the scientist directly. As she
pointed out in her April 21 story:

> Under the terms of her accreditation to report on the activities of MET
> Alpha, this reporter was not permitted to interview the scientist or
> visit his home. Nor was she permitted to write about the discovery of

the scientist for three days, and the copy was then submitted for a check by military officials.

Those officials asked that details of what chemicals were uncovered be deleted. They said they feared that such information could jeopardize the scientist's safety by identifying the part of the weapons program where he worked.

…While this reporter could not interview the scientist, she was permitted to see him from a distance at the sites where he said that material from the arms program was buried.

Clad in nondescript clothes and a baseball cap, he pointed to several spots in the sand where he said chemical precursors and other weapons material were buried.

Let's call this character "Yankee Fan," on account of his baseball cap and his apparent helpfulness to the Americans. Miller claims she was not allowed to interview Yankee Fan and that her story was reviewed by the military before publication. Yet given her admission the following day, the claim that she didn't speak to Yankee Fan is awfully suspicious.

In a television interview on PBS's *NewsHour* with Jim Lehrer the following day, April 22, Miller celebrated the Yankee Fan story as a "silver bullet" and "more than a smoking gun" that validated the administration's case for war. Then she went on to describe him as "an Iraqi individual, a scientist, as we've called him."[49] *A scientist, as we've called him.* Miller and her unit, it seems, had made a conscious decision to label him a scientist, which made him seem credible and authoritative. She would refer to him as a scientist again on April 23 and 24. Yet, in a recap article three months later, Miller would admit he was really an Iraqi intelligence officer.[50]

There's a sad irony to the military and Miller presenting an intelligence officer as a scientist to support claims about WMD. One of the key accusations the United States made against Iraq when discussing its policy of "denial and deception" was that Iraq had intelligence officers pose as scientists to answer the questions of weapons inspectors. Effectively, by labeling Yankee Fan a scientist, the military was doing the same thing the United States accused Saddam of doing.

If there were any doubts about Miller misleading her readers about the identity of Yankee Fan, they were erased later by one of her editors. In an e-mail to *The Nation*'s Russ Baker in June 2003, the *Times*'s assistant managing editor, Andrew Rosenthal, assured Baker that "Judy Miller was aware of his identity and in fact met him, but was asked to withhold his name out of concern for his personal safety."[51]

In September 2004, the Duelfer Report shed some light on the substance of Yankee Fan's claims. The report presented the findings of the Iraq Survey Group (ISG), the larger, more specialized group that replaced the 75th XTF in June 2003 as the primary weapons-hunting unit. Named after the leader of the ISG, Charles Duelfer, the report is considered the definitive statement on Iraq's WMDs.

It described a number of site visits conducted by an exploitation team that matched Miller's description of her unit's visits led by Yankee Fan. According to the report, these site visits, conducted in April 2003, discovered a lab that was shut down two days before the beginning of the war; a lab in a house, the chemical preparation division's final location, at which the weapons search team found buried chemicals; a vast warehouse complex, with two relatively intact laboratories where another lab had been burned down in March 2003, according to a Mukhabarat or Iraqi Intelligence Service (IIS) officer; and one last site, with equipment for testing on animals and still more buried chemicals.[52] In short, the Duelfer Report corroborated some aspects of Yankee Fan's story.

But on the key claim—that these chemicals were precursors related to a chemical weapons program—the Duelfer Report did not corroborate the story. At each of these sites, the report said, the chemicals found either were not related to chemical weapons, or the exploitation team did not test them:

> In April 2003 an exploitation team…found IIS documents and a few laboratory-related items and chemicals, but nothing appeared to be CBW [chemical and biological weapons] related.… The specific chemicals were not detailed in the exploitation report, but no CW agents

were present in the warehouses.... The team determined that sample analysis would be unfeasible, so the identity of the chemicals remains unknown.[53]

Further, a Mukhabarat officer associated with these site visits appeared to have been overselling his knowledge of the sites. According to the report, the officer described "the chemical components in non-scientific terms, such as 'impressive and beautiful,' which indicates that he probably has little training in chemistry and may not have had direct knowledge about the identity of the chemicals."[54] This may or may not be Yankee Fan. But, clearly, someone without expertise in the matter was making claims about these finds. And finally, as the Duelfer Report concluded more generally, any chemical activities that had been found were small-scale research projects, not large-scale weapons projects.

In short, Yankee Fan gave Miller's unit something much less than a silver bullet. The sites he showed them had nothing to do with biological and chemical warfare. The destruction of evidence relating to a small research program did nothing to explain the absence of the large-scale WMD programs the administration used to sell the war. And despite Yankee Fan's claim that Iraqis cooperated with Al Qaeda, a Senate report concluded in 2006 that there have only ever been three attempted contacts between Iraq and Al Qaeda, not the cooperation he described.[55]

\* \* \*

In getting a lot of her big stories in Iraq, Judith Miller had help from Ahmed Chalabi. As Miller pointed out in a note to John Burns, the *Times*'s bureau chief in Baghdad, she had known and written about Chalabi for a decade, and "he has provided most of the front page exclusives on WMD to our paper."[56]

Chalabi, the charismatic head of the Iraqi National Congress, was the Iraqi opposition leader favored by the Pentagon and by Vice President Cheney's office to head a new government in Iraq after Saddam Hussein's removal, a government that would be friendly to the United States and Israel. Chalabi had longstanding affiliations with leading neoconservatives, having met Richard Perle and Paul Wolfowitz in the late 1960s while he was getting his Ph.D. in theoretical mathematics at the University of Chicago. In the year leading up to the war, Chalabi and the INC contracted with the Pentagon's Defense Intelligence Agency (DIA) to offer information on Iraq — and, effectively, to create propaganda in support of the war. Chalabi provided a stream of exiles who would tell the intelligence community (or, just as often, the American media, especially Miller) precisely what the hawks in the Bush administration wanted them to hear.

But Chalabi also caused deep divisions among the administration. He had worked with the CIA in the mid-1990s, until the CIA blamed him for a coup attempt gone awry and refused to work with him. The State Department had soured on Chalabi's INC after an audit proved much of the money had disappeared or gone to fancy offices. Indeed, one of the fiercest battles of the Iraq War occurred between the Defense and State departments over who should rule Iraq, Chalabi or a more broad-based group including those who had survived in Iraq under Saddam.

When Chalabi arrived in Iraq after the invasion, he and Miller continued their past working relationship, with Chalabi providing her exclusive stories. Miller says there was "absolutely no connection" between Yankee Fan and Chalabi, even though Yankee Fan made some of the same unsubstantiated claims as many INC defectors of an Iraqi–Al Qaeda connection.[57] But the public affairs officer in Miller's unit, Eugene Pomeroy, seemed to link Chalabi and Yankee Fan. On the same day (April 21) that Miller's Yankee Fan story was published, Miller wrote to Pomeroy, objecting to a military order for her and MET Alpha to return to Talil from Baghdad:

> The hunt for WMD is here, not in Talil. I'm assigned to cover that hunt. I want to remain here in Baghdad without disembedding until MET Alpha returns to Baghdad with the 75th XTF, when I shall rejoin them. I see no reason for me to waste time (or Met Alpha, for that matter) in Talil…. request permission to stay on here with ~~Ahmad Cha~~ colleagues at the Palestine Hotel till Met Alpha returns or order to return is

rescinded. I intend to write about this decision in the NYTimes to send a successful team back…just as progress on WMD is being made.[58]

As authors Michael Isikoff and David Corn point out in *Hubris*, Miller crossed out Chalabi's name in her note, preferring to hide that she was lobbying to stay with Chalabi.[59]

Pomeroy was clearly irked by Miller's note:

> The journalist is here as an observer. If you want to run around with Ahmed Chalabi, looking for baseball-hatted scientists, that's your business. But to interfere with the operations of a military unit, that's unconscionable.[60]

But Miller appealed to General David Petraeus, who suggested to the commander of the unit that he rescind the order, which he did. Thus it happened that a civilian journalist overrode military orders so her team could remain in Baghdad working with Chalabi.

And Chalabi provided Miller with several good stories. On April 21, Chalabi turned over Saddam's son-in-law to MET Alpha, Miller's unit. The move violated Army practices on interrogation, but, as Chalabi's spokesperson Zaab Sethna explained, it was a "good story," and it provided Miller's unit with an opportunity to look heroic, taking custody of one of Saddam's family members.[61] On April 27, Miller wrote of her interview with the father of Iraq's anthrax program, Nassir Hindawi, who had taken refuge with Chalabi. These articles, along with the two articles citing Yankee Fan, created the appearance of progress with the WMD hunt.

*       *       *

The Miller-Chalabi relationship was a two-way street. On at least one occasion, Miller helped Chalabi fight his battles for influence within Iraq.

On April 28, Burns, the *Times* bureau chief in Baghdad, told Miller another *Times* reporter was working on a major profile of Chalabi.[62] At the time, various opposition leaders were jockeying for power in the new assembly, and Chalabi's conviction for embezzlement in Jordan was being raised to discredit him. Lucky for him, then, that Miller managed to get her own profile of Chalabi published in the *Times* on May 1, effectively preempting her colleague's profile. Burns wrote Miller an e-mail chastening her for preempting the other article: "I am deeply chagrined at your reporting and filing on Chalabi after I had told you on Monday night that we were planning a major piece on him—and without so much as telling me what you were doing."[63]

Miller was not apologetic, and she responded by pointing out her decade-long relationship with Chalabi. The exchange revealed her aggressiveness, her lack of consideration of her co-workers—and that she was hell-bent on getting her friendly profile of Chalabi in the paper. The reason may have been that Miller's profile contained a hit against Chalabi's rival.

Miller's article focused on Chalabi's campaign to prohibit Baath party members from retaining any power in the new Iraqi government. Under Saddam's regime, all government functionaries had had to belong to the ruling Baath party. But the process of de-Baathification (led as it would be by Chalabi and his nephew) turned out to be a way to dictate who got to participate in the new government and who didn't.

Miller's profile used the shield of de-Baathification to attack a Chalabi rival named Saad al-Janabi. Like Chalabi, Janabi came from a prominent Iraqi family, enjoyed financial success while in exile, and had set up a kind of power brokerage in Baghdad; but unlike Chalabi, who is a Shia Muslim, Janabi is a Sunni. Janabi had recently returned to Iraq from exile in California and was a critic and rival of Chalabi. Miller's article included information—attributed to anonymous sources—that attacked Janabi's reputation directly:

> Mr. Chalabi declined to name names, but other representatives of the Iraqi National Congress said that the Central Intelligence Agency had retained Saad Janabi as a key advisor. The opposition members identified Mr. Janabi as a former assistant to Hussein Kamel, Mr. [Saddam] Hussein's son-in-law who oversaw weapons programs, defected to

Jordan in 1995, and was killed by Mr. Hussein's government when he later returned to Iraq.

A C.I.A. spokesman in Washington said he had no comment on whether Mr. Janabi was advising the agency.

As an assistant to Hussein Kamel, Janabi certainly was closely placed to Saddam Hussein before he left Iraq in 1995. But Kamel's most significant act was not his marriage to Saddam's daughter but his defection from Iraq in 1995 and his subsequent claim to international weapons inspectors that all the WMD programs had been destroyed—a claim we now know to be correct. Janabi's affiliation with Kamel should have marked him as a formerly well-connected Baathist who had broken with Saddam irrevocably eight years earlier. Instead, Miller's story implicated Janabi as a Baathist.

It's not clear what connection Janabi had with the CIA.[64] A *Times* report from later in the summer suggested he had helped the CIA persuade Iraqi generals to defect.[65] And even the first head of the Iraqi reconstruction, Jay Garner, believed Janabi was "under the employment of the U.S. government." Whether or not that made him an asset, the accusation was certain to cool Janabi's reception in Iraq—if not endanger his life.

So Chalabi's INC, a close ally of Vice President Cheney's office, used Miller to reveal the CIA affiliation of a rival candidate in Iraq. Weeks later, the vice president's office would employ a similar tactic, giving Miller an exclusive leak that would lead to the exposure of another CIA affiliation—but this time with the aim of hurting an administration opponent at home in the United States.

\* \* \*

Less than a week after Miller's Chalabi profile, he offered her another one of his "good stories" which diverted attention from the lack of WMDs—a remarkable trek into the flooded basement of Iraq's intelligence headquarters. "We thought this was a great story for *The New York Times*," Chalabi spokesman Zaab Sethna said of the incident.[66] On May 7, an INC employed Mukhabarat officer brought MET Alpha on a search for a seventh-century Talmud. Miller described the excursion using evocative language right out of *Indiana Jones:*

> The group arrived at Mukhabarat headquarters only to find the section of the building in which the precious document was said to be stored under four feet of murky, fetid water. Dead animals floated on the surface. The stairwell down to the muck was littered with shards of glass, pieces of smashed walls and other bombing debris.
>
> Temporarily daunted by the overpowering stench, MET Alpha's leader, Chief Warrant Officer Richard L. Gonzales, and two other MET Alpha soldiers eventually collected themselves and plunged into the mire in search of the holy text as the team chaplain shook his head in disbelief.

Miller's surreal descriptions continued, setting the stage for the discovery of an even more bizarre set of objects: a collection of items suggesting that Iraq continued to scout out Israel for attack. There was a mock-up of the Israeli parliament, the Knesset; a map marking the Scud missile hits Iraq had made on Israel during the first Gulf War; and a satellite picture of Israel's nuclear reactor, Dimona. In addition, the team found a range of books and historical texts on Jewish culture and a book by Miller's mentor, the Princeton University professor Bernard Lewis.

And then, while hunting for an ancient Talmud in the basement, Miller's team somehow found evidence of a rejected uranium offer in an entirely different part of the building:

> Of even greater interest to MET Alpha was a "top secret" intelligence memo found in a room on another floor. Written in Arabic and dated May 20, 2001, the memo from the Iraqi intelligence station chief in an African country described an offer by a "holy warrior" to sell uranium and other nuclear material. The bid was rejected, the memo states, because of the United Nations "sanctions situation." But the station chief wrote that the source was eager to provide similar help at a more convenient time.[67]

There's a lot that's weird about this find, besides the floating animal carcasses and the mock-up of the Knesset. Miller gave the reader the impression that this excursion was one of the first into the Mukhabarat; in fact, Chalabi's associates had already removed *sixty tons* of documents from the Mukhabarat.[68] She didn't reveal the presence of Pentagon advisor Harold Rhode, a key architect of the alternative intelligence collection programs that justified the war.[69] And then, two days later, she wrote that much of the evidence had simply disappeared, apparently removed by a looter in the interim day.

But the story did give Miller an opportunity to highlight the memo alleging an offer to sell uranium. The memo might be taken as evidence that Iraq was fulfilling UN sanctions; or it could be taken as an explanation for why Iraq never finalized the Niger uranium purchase. But it also suggested that someone with ties to Islamic extremism, perhaps even someone with ties to Al Qaeda, offered Saddam uranium.[70] And the document also supported administration claims that Saddam was in contact with African countries in addition to Niger about uranium. As bizarre as Miller's Mukhabarat story was, it might have proved useful to the administration had the story not appeared just as increased attention focused on the Niger claims.

\*   \*   \*

But Miller's truly heroic efforts to sustain the administration's WMD claims came when she helped present the case that trailers discovered in Iraq were the mobile bioweapons labs (MBLs) that Chalabi's defectors had described before the war, which served as the basis for Bush's and Powell's MBL claims.

On May 8, while still in Baghdad, Miller reported that coalition forces had found a trailer on April 19 that might be an MBL. Again relying largely on anonymous sources and one named source, Miller wrote that the trailer matched the description given by Curveball, the defector who described MBLs to German intelligence:

"While some of the equipment on the trailer could have been used for purposes other than biological weapons agent production, U.S. and U.K. technical experts have concluded that the unit does not appear to perform any function beyond what the defector said it was for, which was the production of biological agents," said Stephen Cambone, the under secretary of defense for intelligence.[71]

Later in the article, however, Miller indicated that experts from the 75th XTF who had inspected the trailer themselves were not so sure. The experts had, by this point, run two sets of tests on samples from the trailer, and the more sophisticated tests showed no trace of biological agents.

In a May 11 story titled "Trailer Is a Mobile Lab Capable of Turning Out Bioweapons, a Team Says," Miller presented a more definitive stance— yet another claim that U.S. forces had found the "smoking gun:"

A team of experts searching for evidence of biological and chemical weapons in Iraq has concluded that a trailer found near Mosul in northern Iraq is a mobile biological weapons laboratory, the three team members said today....

[The team leader] contended that this could be construed as the kind of "smoking gun" that his team was charged with finding to substantiate the Bush administration's allegations that Iraq was making biological and chemical weapons.

Doubters remained, however:

The members acknowledged that some experts were still uncertain whether the trailer was intended to produce biological agents. But they said they were persuaded that it was a mobile lab for biological production.

There was one big problem with Miller's story: The team members didn't address the explanation offered by the Iraqis, which was that the trailer was for producing hydrogen for weather balloons, although they did discount some fairly absurd alternatives, such as that the trailer was a nuclear reactor on wheels. And Miller, the veteran reporter on WMDs, somehow didn't find such an explanation implausible, nor the idea that a trailer with no shock absorbers might be declared a mobile laboratory.

The timing of Miller's May 11 article had a purpose, it seems: She produced the report on the same day a three-person team of CIA experts arrived in Baghdad to assess the trailers. Before the new team even began its examination, the paper of record had declared the trailers to be MBLs.

The administration would again preempt the next assessment of the trailers. On May 16, 2003, the CIA produced a white paper summarizing its findings about the MBLs. Published under the direction of Deputy Director John McLaughlin, the white paper claimed that the trailers met Curveball's description of the MBLs.[72] The trailer, it explained, "is strikingly similar to descriptions provided by a source who was a chemical engineer that managed one of the mobile plants." There were inconsistencies, however. Though Curveball had described a trailer with hydraulic support legs, this trailer was based on an army tank transporter with no hydraulics; the trailer had a cooling unit not originally described by Curveball; and the trailer had three pumps, not the eighteen initially described by Curveball. The white paper dismissed those inconsistencies by arguing that the MBLs were a "newer prototype."

The white paper didn't mention (though a later Miller and William Broad article did)[73] that there was no way to sterilize or drain the central processing tank in the trailer. As for the Iraqi claim that the trailers served to make hydrogen balloons, a claim that was backed by an abundance of evidence, the white paper simply dismissed it as more "denial and deception": "The Iraqis have used sophisticated denial and deception methods that include the use of cover stories that are designed to work."

The white paper failed to consider the main objections to the theory that the trailers were MBLs. Yet it used absolute language—"the strongest evidence to date that Iraq was hiding a biological warfare program"—to describe its findings. In short, the white paper was a profound act of dishonesty that dismissed inconsistencies yet never considered the most obvious explanations.

On May 19, the White House was briefed on the paper. The briefing was then leaked to Miller and Broad, and they published an article about it on May 21. Once more, the article quoted anonymous officials declaring definitively that the trailers were MBLs:

> United States intelligence agencies have concluded that two mysterious trailers found in Iraq were mobile units to produce germs for weapons, but they have found neither biological agents nor evidence that the equipment was used to make such arms, according to senior administration officials.

The *Times* article also announced—as an Associated Press article had the day before—that the Jefferson Project, a team made up of international experts on bioweapons and sponsored by the Pentagon's Defense Intelligence Agency (DIA), was convening in Kuwait; the team would investigate the trailer on May 25 and 26. This appeared to be another case of preemptive leaking to Miller to undercut the impending work of real experts and analysts.

As it turned out, the Jefferson Project team strongly disagreed with the white paper "consensus." In an e-mail summary sent back to the United States on May 27, the team refuted most of the earlier conclusions about the trailers. The Jefferson Project certified that the Iraqis' explanation—that the trailer had served to produce hydrogen weather balloons—was plausible.[74] And it dismissed outright the possibility that the trailers were MBLs: "The trailer could not be used as a transportable biological production system as the system is currently configured."

By this point, however, Miller and Broad's May 21 article had already preempted the Jefferson Project results, and the group's e-mailed summary would not circulate formally outside of the DIA until the following year. Nevertheless, the administration took one more step to ensure the white paper would remain unchallenged by the Jefferson Project results: the CIA declassified the white paper on May 28, *the day after* the Jefferson Project results came in, and sponsored a briefing for the press.

Yet results of the Jefferson Project leaked. For a June 7 article laying out many of the doubts about the trailers, Miller and Broad referred to a third assessment (presumably the Jefferson Project) in which "more senior analysts divided sharply over the function of the trailers." But those doubts were largely dismissed by the CIA and top administration officials. What mattered, for an administration anxious to provide some validation for its case for war, was that the careful timing of its document leaks and releases worked. By first getting its desired MBL interpretations publicized and then declassifying the white paper, the administration generated enough "news" to drown out any alternative interpretations. And Miller and the *Times* had helped carry the message.

On May 29, based on the white paper, a twelve-day-old document refuted by more recent inspections by international experts, President George W. Bush publicly proclaimed—at a summit in Poland—that coalition forces had found WMD:

> We found the weapons of mass destruction. We found biological laboratories. You remember when Colin Powell stood up in front of the world, and he said, Iraq has got laboratories, mobile labs to build biological weapons. They're illegal. They're against the United Nations resolutions, and we've so far discovered two. And we'll find more weapons as time goes on. But for those who say we haven't found the banned manufacturing devices or banned weapons, they're wrong. We found them.[75]

# CHAPTER 3

# TRUTH AND CONSEQUENCES

(July 2003)

---

*Democracy asks us, requires us, to be engaged with issues, to become involved and not to accede to the loudest voices without questioning them.*
—Joseph Wilson, *The Politics of Truth*

As the Iraq War passed into its third and fourth months, the looting that immediately followed the invasion gave way to more dangerous chaos—the rise of a Sunni insurgency targeting U.S. troops. The administration's rosy scenario of Iraqis greeting American soldiers as liberators never materialized. The U.S. management structure in Iraq underwent its own crisis: In an effort to boost the authority of the top U.S. leader in Iraq and install a person he trusted, Defense Secretary Donald Rumsfeld orchestrated the replacement of Jay Garner—who had led initial reconstruction efforts—with Paul Bremer, who was to head the new Coalition Provisional Authority (CPA). American forces had found neither Saddam Hussein nor the WMDs used to justify the war.

Back at home, the questions about WMDs got more and more insistent as Iraq grew more and more unstable. Democrats demanded an investigation into the WMD claims.[76] Reporters posed increasingly challenging questions about why no WMDs had been found more than three months after the invasion. Lots of reports debunking the MBL claims came out.[77]

At the same time, the claim that Iraq had tried to buy five hundred tons of uranium from Niger in 1999 came under increasing scrutiny. On May 6,

*The New York Times*'s Nicholas Kristof wrote a column citing an anonymous ambassador who had traveled to Niger and discredited the intelligence about Iraq's uranium deal. And in a June 12 *Washington Post* story, Walter Pincus said the unnamed envoy had proved the intelligence wrong.

But the true blow to the administration came on July 6, 2003, when Joseph C. Wilson, the former ambassador to São Tomé and Gabon, published an op-ed in the *Times* titled "What I Didn't Find in Africa." The opening lines went straight for the jugular:

> Did the Bush administration manipulate intelligence about Saddam Hussein's weapons programs to justify an invasion of Iraq?
>
> Based on my experience with the administration in the months leading up to the war, I have little choice but to conclude that some of the intelligence related to Iraq's nuclear weapons program was twisted to exaggerate the Iraqi threat.[78]

Wilson went on to describe a trip he made in February 2002—as a result of an inquiry Vice President Dick Cheney made to the CIA—to determine if there was any truth to the Niger uranium claims. Wilson spent eight days in Niger, talking to former government officials about the country's uranium mines, and learned that it would be almost impossible for Iraq to make a five-hundred-ton uranium deal without the international consortium that operated the mines learning of the sale. Furthermore, such a deal would require the signatures of at least two top Nigerien officials. As Wilson explained, "there's simply too much oversight over too small an industry for a sale to have transpired."

A credible former ambassador was publicly confirming the doubts many had raised anonymously.[79] Here was concrete evidence supporting the suspicion that the administration gamed the intelligence to justify the war.

\* \* \*

A Californian by birth and heritage, Wilson spent much of his teens in France, where his parents were journalists. The experience left him with an appreciation for foreign cultures and a fluency in French. Following graduation in 1971 from the University of California, Santa Barbara, and after an accident ended his short carpentry career, Wilson passed the Foreign Service exam. He hoped he might get sent to Europe, but instead ended up in the former French colony of Niger. He served in several more African countries, including Congo and South Africa, both uranium producers, before he was named deputy chief of mission to Iraq in 1988.

When Saddam Hussein invaded Kuwait in August 1990, the U.S. ambassador to Iraq, April Glaspie, was in the United States on home leave. That left Wilson as the most senior official in Baghdad, responsible for the safety of a hundred Americans at the embassy and more held captive by the Iraqis. In a surprise meeting, Wilson stared down a gun-toting Saddam Hussein and criticized him for closing the borders, effectively holding civilians hostage. Weeks later, when the Iraqis ordered that all people who had taken sanctuary would have to register in person with the Iraqi government under penalty of death, Wilson showed up at his morning press briefing wearing a noose as a necktie. As he said, "If he wants to execute me for keeping Americans from being taken hostage, I will bring my own fucking rope."[80] The Iraqis eventually withdrew the order. For his service in Iraq, President George H. W. Bush celebrated Wilson as a "true American hero."

After the Gulf War, Wilson served as ambassador to Gabon (another uranium producer) and São Tomé and Principe. He then served in President Bill Clinton's White House as senior director of African affairs. In 1998, Wilson married Valerie Plame, whom he had fallen in love with at first sight when they met in 1997 at a reception in Washington, D.C. At the time, Wilson was the political advisor to the European Command, and Plame told him she was an energy executive working out of Brussels. In fact, as he later found out, she was a CIA spy. Plame's cover was known in Agency parlance as non-official cover (NOC); it is the most delicate kind of cover, because it doesn't carry the protection of a diplomatic passport. Posing as an energy executive, Plame developed contacts within the world of nuclear proliferation. Because Wilson had security clearance, Plame was able to reveal her cover to him before their relationship turned serious and they were married.

In July 1998, Wilson retired after twenty-three years of service in the diplomatic corps. Yet he still served the cause of diplomacy. The following year, Nigerien president Ibrahim Baré Maïnassara, who had assumed power after a coup in 1996, invited Wilson to help him cede power to civilian rule. As it happened, Maïnassara didn't survive long enough to cede power—he was assassinated in April 1999. Not long after, Wilson returned to Niger and, at the urging of Prime Minister Ibrahim Mayaki, coached Maïnassara's successor to cede power himself. That same year the CIA sent Wilson to Niger to investigate allegations that Abdul Qadeer Khan, the Pakistani nuclear scientist and broker, was pursuing uranium in Niger, though Wilson's trip didn't generate any new information on Khan.[81]

Between Wilson's experience in Africa and his knowledge of Saddam Hussein, he was eminently qualified to go to Niger to find out whether the Iraqis had tried to buy yellowcake from Niger. The idea to send him came up at a discussion of counterproliferation professionals. They had received an inquiry from Cheney for more information on the Niger allegations and were trying to figure out how they could confirm or deny the report. Someone remembered Wilson's 1999 trip, so they asked Valerie Plame Wilson, who by now worked out of Washington, D.C., on the Joint Iraq Task Force, to summarize his qualifications for the trip.[82] "My husband has good relations with both the PM and the former Minister of Mines (not to mention lots of French contacts), both of which could possibly shed light on this sort of activity," she wrote.

On February 19, 2002, these counterproliferation officers invited Joe Wilson to a meeting at the CIA headquarters. His wife introduced him and left, after which those present discussed how Wilson might be able to help. Douglas Rohn, a State Department Bureau of Intelligence and Research (INR) analyst on Africa, took his own notes of the meeting. He wrote:

> Meeting apparently convened by Valerie Wilson, a CIA WMD managerial type, and the wife of Amb. Joe Wilson, with the idea that the agency and the larger USG could dispatch Joe to Niger to use his contacts there to sort out the Niger/Iraq sale question.[83]

Because he arrived late, Rohn mistakenly overemphasized Valerie Wilson's role as having "apparently convened" the meeting.[84] That minor inaccuracy was compounded later when his notes served as the basis for a memo, produced by INR at the request of Under Secretary of State Marc Grossman, that stated her role more definitively—"convened by Valerie Wilson," with no qualification. The memo would in turn form the basis for administration claims that she sent her husband to Niger.

Later that month, Joe Wilson traveled to Niger, meeting first with U.S. Ambassador Barbro Owens-Kirkpatrick in Niamey, who told him she had already made several inquiries and had determined there was no substance to the yellowcake allegations.[85] Wilson then reached out to Nigerien businessmen and former government officials, including Mai Manga, the minister of mines at the time of the alleged uranium deal. Manga said there hadn't been a sale of uranium outside of International Atomic Energy Agency (IAEA) oversight since the 1980s, adding that it would be almost impossible to bypass the French consortium that ran the mines. Wilson met with former prime minister Ibrahim Mayaki, who reported that no contracts had been signed while he was prime minister, which covered some of the period of the alleged deal. But he did admit to one contact with an Iraqi. At a meeting in 1999 of the Organization of African Unity in Algiers, an Iraqi businessman (actually Mohammed Saeed al-Sahaf, Saddam's propaganda minister, better known as Baghdad Bob) had approached him about expanding trade relations. Mayaki avoided the discussion, worrying about the sanctions against Iraq. So he never learned precisely what Baghdad Bob wanted. But he assumed it might have had to do with uranium.[86]

When Wilson returned on March 5, he didn't write a report on the trip himself. Instead, two CIA officers debriefed him that night. A reports officer who had not attended the February 19 meeting then summarized Wilson's findings. As in a game of telephone, that report gave a much different emphasis on matters than Wilson believed he had given. Wilson says that he detailed for the CIA officers the names of people who would be involved in any Nigerien uranium sale, but the report focused instead on the meeting between Baghdad Bob and Mayaki.[87] To make matters worse, the reports officer seems to have recorded (and believed) that the meeting took place in Niger, when in fact it occurred in Algiers.[88] Because of that misunderstanding, the reports officer took this as confirmation of reports from the forged Italian documents that Wissam al-Zahawie, Iraq's ambassador to the Vatican, traveled to Niger to seek uranium in 1999.

The introduction of this error would contribute to the inconsistent treatment of the report on Wilson's trip over time. When the report was released, "no one believed it added a great deal of new information to the Iraq-Niger uranium story."[89] As a result, it was not used to support or refute the Niger allegations, at least not for a while.

But the administration's arguments about the substance of this intelligence would change over time. When the White House first drafted speeches in the fall of 2002, it implied it had interrupted an almost-completed Iraq–Niger uranium deal. For example, the draft of the October 7 Cincinnati speech claimed, "The [Iraqi] regime has been caught attempting to purchase up to 500 metric tons of uranium oxide from Africa."[90] During this time, the administration never used the report from Wilson's trip to support the claim. But when Bush gave his State of the Union speech a few months later, it made a much weaker claim: that Iraq had "sought" uranium.[91] By weakening the claim, the administration could still use the false insinuations about al-Zahawie's trip to justify war on Iraq—and it could also now use the report from Wilson's trip. So when the IAEA asked on February 4 if the United States had anything to support its claims other than the intelligence based on the forgeries, and when Rumsfeld asked on March 8 if the Niger uranium claim remained valid after the forgeries were exposed, the government twice cited the report from Wilson's trip as evidence that Iraq had "sought" uranium from Niger.[92]

Wilson never saw the trip report, so he had no way of knowing that it didn't reflect his understanding of the conversation.

\*   \*   \*

Since the summer of 2002, Wilson had contributed to the debates on Iraq. He was not antiwar per se, but based on his experience with Saddam, he believed it would be more effective to make disarmament—not "regime change"—the goal of any authorization to use force, because doing so would play to Saddam's instinct for self-preservation rather than provoking him into fighting back. Wilson made that case in an op-ed he wrote in October 2002 for the *San Jose Mercury News:*

> "Regime change" as a rationale for military action will ensure that Saddam will use every weapon in his arsenal to defend himself.... But history also shows that the less-confrontational approach favored by some on the Security Council—France and Russia—isn't likely to work, either. Saddam has, after all, repeatedly flouted UN resolutions and ignored its demands to let weapons inspectors back into the country for almost four years.... One of the strongest arguments for a militarily supported inspection plan is that it doesn't threaten Saddam with extinction, a threat that could push him to fight back with the very weapons we're seeking to destroy. If disarmament is the goal, Saddam can be made to understand that only his arsenal is at stake, not his survival.[93]

Wilson wrote that President Bush's father "agreed with almost everything" in the article, while former national security advisor Brent Scowcroft asked for permission to "take it over to the White House," which Wilson took to mean he would share it with national security advisor Condoleezza Rice or with her deputy, Stephen Hadley.[94]

Wilson made three direct attempts to get the administration to correct the record on the Niger allegations. On January 28, 2003, when Wilson heard Bush mention uranium from Africa in his State of the Union speech, he called a friend at the State Department to find out whether the line was referring to the Niger claim Wilson believed he had debunked; the friend assumed the reference related to another African nation. Then, after Wilson saw Rice on national television on June 8, claiming "nobody in my circles" knew the Niger intelligence was bad, Wilson was mystified. He called a close Rice associate to try to get her to correct the record. Finally, he had another conversation with a senior official at the State Department, again trying to correct the record. That official replied that Wilson would probably have to correct the record himself.

Which is what Joe Wilson set out to do when he wrote the July 6 op-ed for the *Times*.

Wilson stepped forward as a citizen to defend the importance of public debate in a democracy—particularly before engaging in war. "America's foreign policy depends on the sanctity of its information," he wrote in the *Times*. He did not step forward as a Democrat or an anti-Bush partisan; he made no mention of political parties.

In his op-ed, Wilson was careful about several points. He explained that his trip arose out of inquiries made by Vice President Cheney, but he did not say Cheney had sent him:

> In February 2002, I was informed by officials at the Central Intelligence Agency that Vice President Dick Cheney's office had questions about a particular intelligence report. While I never saw the report, I was told that it referred to a memorandum of agreement that documented the sale of uranium yellowcake—a form of lightly processed ore— by Niger to Iraq in the late 1990's.

Wilson also made clear that he had not seen what we now know to be forgeries:

> As for the actual memorandum, I never saw it. But news accounts have pointed out that the documents had glaring errors—they were signed, for example, by officials who were no longer in government—and were probably forged.

Wilson noted he had not written a report on the trip itself. But he explained, based on his experience in the Clinton White House, that "there should be at least four documents in United States government archives confirming my mission." Finally, Wilson also admitted the possibility that his report had been deemed inaccurate. In short, Wilson's op-ed was a fairly carefully worded account of his involvement in attempts to ascertain whether the Niger allegations were true.

But Wilson also posed a very dangerous question for an administration that had ignored warnings about its central argument for war: "Did the Bush administration manipulate intelligence about Saddam Hussein's weapons programs to justify an invasion of Iraq?"

Wilson's question might not have been perceived as such a threat if it weren't for the two articles that appeared prior to his op-ed that used Wilson as an anonymous source. In a May 6 column in the *Times*, Nicholas Kristof suggested Dick Cheney's office had sent Wilson:

> I'm told by a person involved in the Niger caper that more than a year ago the vice president's office asked for an investigation of the uranium deal, so a former U.S. ambassador to Africa was dispatched to Niger.[95]

And it stated flatly that Wilson had exposed the Niger documents as forgeries:

> In February 2002, according to someone present at the meetings, that envoy reported to the C.I.A. and State Department that the information was unequivocally wrong and that the documents had been forged.

A June 12 article by Walter Pincus in the *Post* also suggested that Wilson had debunked the forgeries:

> After returning to the United States, the envoy reported to the CIA that the uranium-purchase story was false, the sources said. Among the envoy's conclusions was that the documents may have been forged because the "dates were wrong and the names were wrong," the former U.S. government official said.[96]

The vice president's office, Wilson was believed to have said, not only ignored the report from his trip but ignored a report debunking the forgeries. In short, thanks to the two articles published beforehand, the question Wilson asked in his op-ed was seen as even more dangerous that it otherwise would have been.

Wilson got maximum mileage out of his op-ed. Richard Leiby of *The Washington Post* published a profile of Wilson on Sunday, July 6—the same day the op-ed appeared. And late that Saturday night, after the op-ed was posted on the *Times*'s website, NBC's *Meet the Press* booked Wilson to appear the next morning. As Wilson had obviously intended, the story began to dominate the news.

The coverage stung the White House all the more because Bush was making an important trip to Africa that week. The press corps focused on Wilson's accusations, and remained focused for most of the week. Bush, Rice, Secretary of State Colin Powell, CIA Director George Tenet, and even British Foreign Secretary Jack Straw were forced to respond to questions about Wilson's op-ed. And so Iraq, not Africa, became the big story of the week.

Over the following weeks, the White House was forced to walk back its claims and acknowledge it had been warned against the "sixteen words" in Bush's speech. In the press gaggle Monday morning before Bush departed for Africa, the White House press secretary, Ari Fleischer, was asked almost twenty questions about Wilson's op-ed, which Fleischer largely dismissed:

> Well, there is zero, nada, nothing new here. Ambassador Wilson, other than the fact that now people know his name, has said all this before.

Nevertheless, Fleischer conceded that Bush's statement in the State of the Union speech was incorrect—and based solely on the Niger forgeries.

> FLEISCHER: The President's statement was based on the predicate of the yellowcake from Niger. The President made a broad statement. So given the fact that the report on the yellowcake did not turn out to be accurate, that is reflective of the President's broader statement, David. So, yes, the President's broader statement was based and predicated on the yellowcake from Niger.

Q: So it was wrong?

FLEISCHER: That's what we've acknowledged with the information on—

Q: The President's statement at the State of the Union was incorrect?

FLEISCHER: Because it was based on the yellowcake from Niger.[97]

Three days later, on July 10, while traveling in Africa, Powell tried to tamp down calls for an apology for using the Niger allegation by insisting the allegation was reasonable. But in so doing, he admitted that one week after Bush's speech in January, Powell himself had found it insufficient for his own UN presentation:

> There was no effort or attempt on the part of the President, or anyone else in the administration, to mislead or to deceive the American people. The President was presenting what seemed to be a reasonable state- ment at that time—and it didn't talk to Niger, it talked specifically about efforts to acquire uranium from nations that had it in Africa....
>
> Subsequently, when we looked at it more thoroughly and when I think it's, oh, a week or two later, when I made my presentation to the United Nations and we really went through every single thing we knew about all of the various issues with respect to weapons of mass destruction, we did not believe that it was appropriate to use that example anymore. It was not standing the test of time. And so I didn't use it, and we haven't used it since.[98]

The next day Rice attempted to end questions about the "sixteen words" by setting up the CIA as a scapegoat. In her press briefing, Rice asserted— three times—that the CIA had cleared the State of the Union speech:

> The CIA cleared the speech.... The CIA cleared the speech in its entirety.... The CIA cleared on it. There was even some discussion on that specific sentence, so that it reflected better what the CIA thought.

And the speech was cleared. Now, I can tell you, if the CIA, the Director of Central Intelligence, had said, take this out of the speech, it would have been gone, without question.[99]

But even while she was deflecting blame onto the CIA, she admitted that the "discussion on that specific sentence" had had to do with the use of the word "Niger":

Q: On that sentence, you said that the CIA changed the—that things were done to accommodate the CIA. What was done?

RICE: Some specifics about amount and place were taken out.

Q: —taken out then?

RICE: Some specifics about amount and place were taken out.

Q: Was "place" Niger?

The CIA cleared the speech. But Rice revealed that it did not clear the use of the reference to Niger.[100]

Later that same day, Tenet took the blame for the speech—kind of:

First, the CIA approved the President's State of the Union address before it was delivered. Second, I am responsible for the approval process in my Agency. And third, the President had every reason to believe that the text presented to him was sound. [101]

But Tenet revealed that in "many speeches" the CIA had avoided the Niger claim because the agency "had questions about some of the reporting." He stressed the fact that the Niger allegation did not show up in the key judgments of the October 2002 National Intelligence Estimate. In fact, the State Department's intelligence service had found the claim "highly dubious."

Rice's scapegoating of Tenet motivated his deputies to dig up some of the memos the CIA wrote in October 2002 warning the White House not to use the Niger claim. This development appeared in a few stories based on leaks about the CIA's warnings. For example, a July 13 *Washington Post* story by Walter Pincus and Mike Allen reported that

> CIA Director George J. Tenet successfully intervened with White House officials to have a reference to Iraq seeking uranium from Niger removed from a presidential speech last October, three months before a less specific reference to the same intelligence appeared in the State of the Union address, according to senior administration officials.[102]

Those stories forced the White House to walk back its claims further. The administration gave two press briefings, the first one on July 18, with the White House communications director, Dan Bartlett, speaking on background, and a second one on July 22 with Rice's deputy, Stephen Hadley, and Bartlett speaking on the record. Between the two briefings, they admitted the CIA had warned them—warned Hadley personally in a conversation over the phone and in two memos—not to use the Niger claim. As Hadley confessed in the July 22 press conference, he had been told in October that the Niger claim was weak. Hadley even provided details that explained just how weak the claim was:

> The amount is in dispute, and it's debatable whether it can be acquired from the source. The CIA memorandum said that it had told—that CIA had told the Congress about concerns about the British claim with respect to this. And finally, the memo noted that Iraq already has 500 metric tons of uranium oxide [yellowcake] in their inventory.[103]

The administration had all but conceded Wilson's point—that the Niger claim shouldn't have been in the State of the Union speech. Wilson had forced the administration to admit that it had used the Niger claim despite being warned against doing so. As he wrote in *The Politics of Truth*, "I told any interested friends and all inquisitive journalists that as my charges had been satisfactorily answered, I'd have nothing more to say."[104]

But the White House was not done with Wilson. It began to attack and discredit him, using two claims he had not made in his op-ed: that Cheney had sent Wilson to Niger and that Wilson had debunked the forged Iraq–Niger documents. Fleischer was the point man for the anti-Wilson campaign, starting on July 7:

> But the fact of the matter is in his statements about the Vice President—the Vice President's office did not request the mission to Niger. The Vice President's office was not informed of his mission and he was not aware of Mr. Wilson's mission until recent press accounts— press reports accounted for it.

On Wednesday, July 9, Fleischer attacked another claim that showed up in the Kristof and Pincus articles, but not in Wilson's op-ed—the claim that Wilson had debunked the forgeries:

> You can ask Ambassador Wilson if he reported that the yellowcake documents were forged. He did not. His report did not address whether the documents were forged or not. His report stated that Niger denied the accusation.

On July 11 and July 12, the White House broadened its attack on Wilson beyond two points he hadn't made, taking on the contents of the report itself. In his statement on July 11, George Tenet provided more details on Wilson's trip, including a description of the confused reporting about Wilson's conversation with Ibrahim Mayaki:

> In an effort to inquire about certain reports involving Niger, the CIA's counterproliferation experts, on their own initiative, asked an individual with ties to the region to make a visit to see what he could learn. He reported back to us that one of the former Nigerien officials he met

stated that he was unaware of any contract being signed between Niger and rogue states for the sale of uranium during his tenure in office. The same former official also said that in June 1999 a businessman approached him and insisted that the former official meet with an Iraqi delegation to discuss "expanding commercial relations" between Iraq and Niger. The former official interpreted the overture as an attempt to discuss uranium sales.... There was no mention in the report of forged documents—or any suggestion of the existence of documents at all.

Tenet repeated the administration talking points: Cheney didn't send Wilson, Wilson didn't mention forgeries. But he added a detail from the classified report on Wilson's trip, precisely the detail that the reports officer seems to have had some confusion about: that Baghdad Bob approached Ibrahim Mayaki to talk about trade relations.

The following day, Fleischer repeated Tenet's story, spinning it in an even more damaging manner. Whether through grammatical sloppiness or deliberate intent, Fleischer suggested that Baghdad Bob approached *Wilson*, not Mayaki, about setting up trade relations between Iraq and Niger, thereby implying Wilson served as a broker between Iraq and Niger.[105] With the attack, Tenet and Fleischer made public the same attempt to repurpose the Wilson trip report that the administration had attempted twice before: that Wilson's report supported, not refuted, the allegations that Iraq was seeking uranium.

*   *   *

There was another White House response to Wilson's op-ed—one even more insidious, though barely noticed. On July 11, both Ari Fleischer and Dan Bartlett made background comments to *Time* magazine's John Dickerson in which they picked up on public comments Fleischer had made claiming that a low-level CIA person was responsible for Wilson's trip. They suggested that Dickerson check out who that low-level person was:

[Fleischer] spoke to me on background about Wilson and the president's amazing decision to blame the CIA. Other reporters wandered in and out of the conversation, but there were stretches where it was just the two of us.... [Fleischer] walked me through all the many problems with Wilson's report: His work was sloppy, contradictory, and hadn't been sanctioned by Tenet or any senior person. Some low-level person at the CIA was responsible for the mission. I was told I should go ask the CIA who sent Wilson....

I chatted with [Bartlett], also on background. We talked about many different aspects of the story—the fight with the CIA, the political implications for the president, and the administration's shoddy damage control. This official also pointed out a few times that Wilson had been sent by a low-level CIA employee and encouraged me to follow that angle.[106]

This was a farce. There wasn't really a "low-level CIA employee" who had sent Wilson; there were, instead, the counterproliferation officers mentioned by Tenet. But Fleischer and Bartlett were pushing the journalists to discover the CIA employee they claimed had sent Wilson. And they were doing it with ominous intent.

# CHAPTER 4

# THE BELTWAY INSIDER

(July–October 2003)

*You could write a book on the bad journalism.* — Robert Novak, *Washington Journal*, C-SPAN, September 15, 2006

Joseph Wilson had single-handedly forced the Bush administration to do something it had not done before or since—admit that it was wrong about a key aspect of the Iraq War. If there was any hope that the Administration would let such an affront drop, that hope was erased on July 14, 2003, when Robert Novak published a column titled "Mission to Niger."

Novak has been a fixture in Washington, D.C., journalism for forty years, most of it as part of a team with Rowland Evans in their newsletter, the *Evans-Novak Political Report.* They specialized, as Novak does still, in inside-the-Beltway tidbits—often just gossip—that offer a glimpse into the inner workings of political power. Novak doesn't hide his grumpy conservative beliefs, though he's not above attacking his own side for a good story. Like Judith Miller of *The New York Times,* Novak has developed a symbiotic relationship with a superb network of sources, although in Novak's case the subject is usually political dirt, which makes his columns nastier and more personal than Miller's stories.

In the 1980s, Novak turned into a one-man media empire, enjoying a weekly syndicated column and a recurring role as a political pundit on CNN shows such as *Crossfire* and *The Capital Gang,* where he pioneered the confrontational clashes that now pass for political commentary. Sometimes known as the "Prince of Darkness," Novak is unapologetic about his trashy brand of insider journalism, in which people leak information to him that will damage their political opponents and Novak knowingly publicizes it.

And that's precisely what happened with his July 14 column, which appeared after the initial excitement surrounding Wilson's July 6 op-ed in the *Times* had seemingly passed. On July 11, CIA director George Tenet had accepted the blame for the allegation about the Iraq-Niger uranium deal having appeared in the State of the Union speech, which temporarily resolved much of the interest in the affair. But Novak's column contained a stealth attack that would, with a helping hand from the White House, revive the whole story.

Novak's column offered yet another backstory to Wilson's trip to Niger. It presented both the CIA and the White House versions of how Wilson got sent to Niger. As White House Press Secretary Ari Fleischer had done the week before, Novak claimed—without attribution—that the decision to send Wilson "was made routinely at a low level without Director George Tenet's knowledge." But Novak also reported a seemingly contradictory claim—"The CIA says its counterproliferation officials selected Wilson and asked his wife to contact him."[107]

In doing so, Novak also distanced Vice President Cheney from any direct role in sparking Wilson's trip: "The White House, State Department and Pentagon, and not just Vice President Dick Cheney, asked the CIA to look into it."[108] Novak then emphasized the importance of the CIA report on Wilson's trip and announced the White House wanted to make it public:

> The story, actually, is whether the administration deliberately ignored Wilson's advice, and that requires scrutinizing the CIA summary of what their envoy reported. The Agency never before has declassified that kind of information, but the White House would like it to do just that now—in its and in the public's interest.[109]

Thus far, then, Novak is simply echoing the Bush administration talking points: Cheney wasn't really behind Wilson's trip, and Wilson's report didn't say what he was now claiming it said. But then he threw in the remarkable sentences that would damage lives and eventually create a national scandal:

Wilson never worked for the CIA, but his wife, Valerie Plame, is an Agency operative on weapons of mass destruction. Two senior administration officials told me Wilson's wife suggested sending him to Niger to investigate the Italian report.

When the Wilsons read that, they knew their lives were changed forever. Valerie Wilson immediately began making a list of things she needed to do to protect her contacts. She had to warn all those she had worked with while undercover that they might be targeted as spies. She worried that her neighbors and friends—who believed her to be an analyst and a soccer mom—would react negatively when they learned the truth. And she knew that she would never again be able to do the work she had loved for many years: helping to keep the United States safe from WMD proliferators. (Ironically, of course, that was precisely what the administration claimed to be doing by going to war against Saddam.)

While Novak's column had a devastating effect on Valerie Wilson's life, the press took little notice of it at the time. David Corn, writing in his blog at *The Nation* on July 16, wondered whether Novak's sources had broken the Intelligence Identities Protection Act (IIPA), a law written in 1982 to prevent the willful exposure of undercover intelligence officers' identities. Tim Phelps and Knut Royce, writing for *Newsday* on July 22, confirmed that Valerie Wilson had worked undercover on WMDs and clarified her role in her husband's trip to Niger:

> A senior intelligence official confirmed that Plame was a Directorate of Operations undercover officer who worked "alongside" the operations officers who asked her husband to travel to Niger.
>
> But he said she did not recommend her husband to undertake the Niger assignment.[110]

Phelps and Royce also quoted Novak on the leak he received: "Novak, in an interview, said his sources had come to him with the information. 'I didn't dig it out, it was given to me,' he said. 'They thought it was significant, they gave me the name and I used it.'" These articles didn't attract much notice. In response to the few questions asked at press briefings, however, the White House categorically denied that anyone at the White House was involved in the leak.

At the CIA, however, the process the agency follows in case of a leak—first determining whether classified information had been leaked, then assessing the damage—had already begun. Based on an initial assessment, the agency notified the Department of Justice (DOJ) on July 30 that a crime might have been committed. After completing its internal review, the CIA requested a DOJ investigation on September 16. And on September 26, 2003, the DOJ decided it would conduct a criminal investigation into circumstances surrounding the leak.

Three days later, *The Washington Post*'s Mike Allen and Dana Priest published an article that raised the stakes. The September 29 article, titled "Bush Administration Is Focus of Inquiry," provided a brief overview of the timing of the leak and the reason—discrediting Joe Wilson—behind it. But then Allen and Priest revealed that the leak had a much greater scope than it first appeared:

> Yesterday, a senior administration official said that before Novak's column ran, two top White House officials called at least six Washington journalists and disclosed the identity and occupation of Wilson's wife. …"Clearly, it was meant purely and simply for revenge," the senior official said of the alleged leak…. It is rare for one Bush administration official to turn on another. Asked about the motive for describing the leaks, the senior official said the leaks were "wrong and a huge miscalculation, because they were irrelevant and did nothing to diminish Wilson's credibility."[111]

The article is commonly referred to by reporters and investigators as the 1x2x6 article, since it suggests one source describing a leak spread by two people to six journalists. The article elevated the importance of the leak—and not just because it revealed dissent within the Bush administration.

For the first time, it now seemed likely that the leakers of Valerie Wilson's identity might be guilty of violating the IIPA, the law criminalizing the deliberate leaking of covert identities.

There are three tests to determine an IIPA violation. First, the leaker must have authorized access to the covert agent's identity and leak that information to someone who is not authorized to receive it.[112] Thus, a White House official with top security clearance could be guilty of violating the law, but Novak and other journalists could not, because they don't have the security clearance. Second, the leaker must be *intentionally* disclosing the information; an accidental revelation is not enough to merit a charge. And finally, the leaker must know the leaked information identifies the covert agent as such.

When the *Post* article quoted an official as saying "it was meant purely and simply for revenge," it implied that the leak was intentional. When it explained that the leakers disclosed the identity and occupation of Valerie Wilson, it suggested the leakers knew she was covert. And when it indicated that the leakers were two "senior administration officials," it implied that they had top security clearance. The three conditions for a possible IIPA violation, it seemed, had been met.

On October 12, the *Post* followed up on its story. The source reiterated the claim, adding the detail that the leak was unsolicited. This made it more likely the leaks would be considered criminal, because it implied that administration officials went out of their way to leak Valerie Wilson's identity.

> The source elaborated on the conversations last week, saying that officials brought up Plame as part of their broader case against Wilson.
>
> "It was unsolicited," the source said. "They were pushing back. They used everything they had."[113]

The October 12 story revealed something else about the leak. It disclosed that a *Post* reporter—whom it did not name—had received a leak about Valerie Wilson:

On July 12, two days before Novak's column, a *Post* reporter was told by an administration official that the White House had not paid attention to the former ambassador's CIA-sponsored trip to Niger because it was set up as a boondoggle by his wife, an analyst with the agency working on weapons of mass destruction. Plame's name was never mentioned and the purpose of the disclosure did not appear to be to generate an article, but rather to undermine Wilson's report.

These stories seemed to support the allegation that there was a deliberate attempt by at least two senior administration officials to leak Wilson's identity to multiple journalists.

After the first *Post* article, on September 29, the White House, through its spokesman, Scott McClellan, denied that anyone in the White House was involved, basically challenging reporters who were covering the story to provide proof of involvement. But there was another, more subtle strategy that emerged that day as well. "If someone leaked classified information of that nature," McClellan stated during a heated press briefing, "then it should be looked into by the Department of Justice." *If* someone leaked *classified* information—the White House was retreating from its categorical denial that anyone had leaked anything, and instead raising doubts that an *intentional* leak of *classified* information had taken place. This was precisely the kind of denial that might get someone out of an IIPA violation.

\*   \*   \*

Once the criminal investigation was announced, Novak had to be concerned that his "two senior administration officials" might be vulnerable to IIPA charges. As Murray Waas would report in the *National Journal* three years later, Novak called Karl Rove on September 29, the day of the 1x2x6 story in the *Post*, to tell him he was going to protect him. "You are not going to get burned.... I don't give up my sources."[114]

Novak and Rove had been down this road before. As President Bush's most important political advisor, Rove had cultivated Bush's career over decades and crafted him into the perfect conservative presidential candidate. Rove is also notorious for using smears and selective leaks to defeat his political enemies. In fact, Rove had gotten in trouble for a leak to Novak in 1992, when the political consultant was providing direct mail services for Bush's father during his presidential reelection campaign. Right after the elder Bush's campaign manager for Texas, Rob Mosbacher, awarded three-quarters of the campaign's direct mail budget to a firm competing with Rove's firm, Novak published a story questioning the effectiveness of Mosbacher's Texas campaign. Novak went on to allege that Mosbacher had been stripped of his authority.[115] Mosbacher figured that only Rove had a motive to leak such an erroneous and damaging story, so he fired Rove from the campaign. So this time, when Novak told Rove he would protect him, the 1992 firing made the terms of the protection clear: As Waas reported, Novak assured Rove, "I'm not going to let that happen to you again."

On October 1, two days after the 1x2x6 piece in the *Post*, Novak published a column that changed or elaborated on key aspects of his July 14 column in ways that seemed to respond to the 1x2x6 article, and specifically to the IIPA law. First, Novak tried to refute the claim that the leak was intentional:

> During a long conversation with a senior administration official, I asked why Wilson was assigned the mission to Niger. He said Wilson had been sent by the CIA's counterproliferation section at the suggestion of one of its employees, his wife. It was an offhand revelation from this official, who is no partisan gunslinger. When I called another official for confirmation, he said: "Oh, you know about it."[116]

This was disingenuous at best, an outright contradiction at worst. In his earlier *Newsday* interview, Novak had said that his sources had "given it to me" and that "they thought it was significant, they gave me the name and I used it." Now he was writing that it was an "offhand revelation" from one official and that the other simply confirmed it. Note too that in his July column Novak had flatly stated that "the CIA says its counterproliferation officials selected Wilson"; now, in October, he was attributing that claim to the first official he talked to.

In the same October 1 column, Novak responded to the "six journalists" claim in the 1x2x6 article:

> The published report that somebody in the White House failed to plant this story with six reporters and finally found me as a willing pawn is simply untrue.[117]

This was not, in fact, what the article had said, but never mind that. Novak seems here to be trying to boost his self-importance by claiming to be the first to have gotten the leak. But, of course, he had no way of knowing whether or not the White House had failed to seed this leak before they spoke to him—unless someone had told him directly.

Novak then tried to refute the notion that Valerie Wilson was covert by suggesting that her identity was well known:

> How big a secret was it? It was well known around Washington that Wilson's wife worked for the CIA. Republican activist Clifford May wrote Monday, in National Review Online, that he had been told of her identity by a non-government source before my column appeared and that it was common knowledge.

Significantly, the über-insider Novak was not claiming he had learned of Valerie Wilson's identity from someone outside government, but reporting that May, a patently partisan source whom investigators would later leave off their list of journalists who had received the leak, had learned it in this way.[118] May, a Republican operative, was making claims that just happened to help Novak and the administration avoid incrimination for an illegal leak.

In support of his claim that Valerie Wilson's name was no secret, Novak also cited *Who's Who:* "Her name, Valerie Plame, was no secret either, appearing in Wilson's 'Who's Who in America' entry." Mind you, Novak didn't claim he got the name Plame from *Who's Who*—only that he *could* have.[119]

Finally, Novak tried to explain away his reference to Valerie Wilson as an "operative":

> A big question is her duties at Langley. I regret that I referred to her in my column as an "operative," a word I have lavished on hack politicians for more than 40 years.

This muddies the issue, however. As Joshua Micah Marshall of talking-pointsmemo.com has shown, when Novak uses the word "operative" in the context of intelligence professionals rather than people working in politics, he is referring to covert officers.[120]

Finally, Novak tried to suggest that Valerie Wilson would not be covered by the IIPA because she was not a covert agent:

> While the CIA refuses to publicly define her status, the official contact says she is "covered"—working under the guise of another agency. However, an unofficial source at the Agency says she has been an analyst, not in covert operations.

As with the *Who's Who* business, this story about Wilson serving as an analyst is a new one. Before the announcement of the investigation and the threat of an IIPA indictment, Novak had never mentioned it. It also provided a convenient prop for McClellan at the White House, responding to inquiries from the press that same day: "And the columnist made it clear he probably shouldn't use that word [covert], because his understanding was that she was, indeed, an analyst. So those are the facts."[121] Taken in total, then, Novak's October column seemed to be an attempt at protecting his White House sources from being susceptible to an IIPA charge, as he apparently promised Rove.

But Novak's seemingly magical coordination with the administration was not over. Neither was his attack on Joe and Valerie Wilson. In an October 4 column, in the guise of discussing Valerie Wilson's political donations to Al Gore, Novak named her CIA front company, an energy outfit called

Brewster & Jennings.[122] Ostensibly, he did so to bolster his argument that Wilson's cover wasn't very well protected, that the company she worked for didn't really exist. Yet by revealing the company's name, Novak had to know that he was exposing more details about Wilson's once-secret cover to a national audience. That same day, two anonymous administration officials, seemingly working off the same talking points as Novak, confirmed to two *Washington Post* journalists that Valerie Wilson had an association with Brewster & Jennings. Remarkably, they had ready at hand Valerie Wilson's personal tax documents—her W-2 forms—to make the confirmation.[123]

Over the course of one week in October 2003, Novak had backed away from his previous column, exposed Valerie Wilson's front company, and insinuated that Wilson's op-ed had been politically motivated. At the end of that week, on October 7, the FBI interviewed Novak about his columns. He reiterated what he wrote on October 1. After Novak was questioned, the FBI asked (and Novak's lawyer recommended) that he remain quiet about his role. From that first interview with the FBI in October 2003 until after Karl Rove escaped charges in 2006, Novak would say almost nothing to the press. But when Novak spoke again, he continued to revise his story on two key issues: The warning the CIA gave him about mentioning Valerie Wilson, and whether his first source intended to leak Valerie Wilson's purported role in her husband's trip.[124]

Bill Harlow, the CIA spokesperson Novak contacted before writing his July 14, 2003, column, claimed in a July 2005 *Washington Post* story that he had given Novak the strongest possible warning not to publish Valerie Wilson's name. In an August 1, 2005, column, Novak attacked Harlow's version, particularly on the issue of whether Harlow had corrected Novak's assertion that Valerie Wilson arranged the trip to Niger. Novak quibbled over the language Harlow had used—Harlow had said "authorized" when Novak had used the term "suggested."[125] But in an interview in 2006, Novak admitted that Harlow had told him that Valerie Plame Wilson had not "suggested" Wilson for the trip: "He told me that Mrs. Wilson did not suggest the mission by her husband, but she was asked to get him to do it by other people in the CIA."[126]

The CIA, Novak acknowledged in 2006, had told him in 2003 that Valerie Wilson did not suggest her husband for the trip. Nevertheless, on the strength of one source who made "an offhand revelation" and another source who simply confirmed whatever it is that Novak said to him, Novak had said exactly that in his notorious July 14, 2003, column: "Two senior administration officials told me Wilson's wife suggested sending him to Niger to investigate the Italian report." Since then, Novak has repeatedly claimed he was justified because the Senate Select Committee on Intelligence (SSCI) report on Iraq's WMD said Plame suggested Joseph Wilson for the Niger mission. The rationalization is a profound act of dishonesty. Novak consistently presents the SSCI judgment as unanimous, when in fact it was anything but.[127] Furthermore, Novak is attempting to justify a claim he made in July 2003 by citing a document published in July 2004. Obviously, the SSCI report can't explain why Novak made the decision to ignore Harlow in 2003.

By Novak's own judgment, publishing the story despite the CIA warning "would be inexcusable for any journalist and particularly a veteran of 48 years in Washington."[128] But it appears he did just that.

Novak backpedaled one more time about his primary source for the July 14, 2003, column. As we saw earlier, shortly after Novak published that column, he claimed both senior administration officials "gave him" Valerie Wilson's name. That fall, he claimed only the first person offered up her role (but not the name), and that that person did so as an "offhand revelation." But in a column published September 14, 2006, Novak said his primary source "did not slip me this information as idle chitchat, as he now suggests. He made clear he considered it especially suited for my column."

With this, Novak has come full circle. First the leak was intentional. Then, in the fall of 2003, when the administration was trying to avoid an IIPA charge, he claimed it was not. And more recently, he has implied it was absolutely intentional. The changes to the story are all the more striking given that intentionality lies at the core of the IIPA statute.

Finally, Novak has never explained the source of one other assertion he made in his column: "Wilson never worked for the CIA." Years later, he said that he used this assertion to frame the question to his first source that elicited the information about Plame. "I asked why the CIA had sent Wilson—who lacked intelligence experience, nuclear policy expertise or recent contact with Niger—on the African mission."[129] But it's not clear how Novak asserted that Wilson had no intelligence background to his primary source without having learned of it first from someone with the clearance to say so. Add that to Novak's unconvincing explanations for his use of the name "Plame" and the word "operative," and his story still doesn't add up.

Perhaps the most generous thing that can be said of Novak's changing stories is what he himself said while on C-SPAN's *Washington Journal:* "My account is close to the truth."[130]

*   *   *

Novak's October 1, 2003, column, the one that works so hard to inoculate his sources against the possibility of an IIPA charge, appears to have had one major consequence. After reading the description of Novak's "primary" source as someone who is "not a partisan gunslinger," Richard Armitage— then deputy secretary of state, and much less involved in the WMD deceptions than the vice president's office or the White House—realized for the first time, he said later, that he was Novak's primary source.[131] He told Secretary of State Colin Powell through the State Department's lawyer and contacted the FBI.[132]

On October 2, Armitage spoke to the FBI without a lawyer. He admitted that in the course of an hour-long interview with Novak on July 8, 2003, he had mentioned that Wilson's wife worked at the CIA and (purportedly) had a role in Wilson's trip, but said he had not known she was covert.[133] He had learned of Valerie Wilson's identity from a memo developed by the State Department's Bureau of Intelligence and Research (INR) after it received requests for more information on Wilson's trip. This was the memo based on Douglas Rohn's inaccurate notes indicating that Valerie Wilson had "convened" the meeting about how to respond to the Niger allegations.

Armitage may have seen a copy of the memo when it was first produced, on June 10, 2003.[134] Then, as Powell prepared for his trip to Africa amid the uproar over Wilson's trip, Armitage called Carl Ford, the head of INR, to request that Powell be brought up to date on Wilson's trip. Ford had someone change the memo slightly, address it anew to Powell, and fax it via secure fax to Air Force One.[135] He also sent a copy to Armitage. Thus, just before Armitage had his interview with Novak on July 8, he had received and read a memo alleging that Valerie Wilson, who worked in WMD at the CIA, "convened" the February 2002 meeting with Joe Wilson at the CIA. When asked in an interview why he passed on the information from a paragraph obviously marked SECRET, Armitage explained he had never seen a covered person's name in a memo before, so he assumed that Valerie Wilson was not undercover.[136] Armitage made an apparently compelling case to the FBI that when he passed on the information to Novak on July 8, he had no idea Valerie Wilson was covert.

Richard Armitage took responsibility for leaking Valerie Wilson's CIA employ to Novak, but he did so on terms that would not make him guilty of an IIPA violation. By coming forward, he made it possible for Novak's chameleon stories to succeed.

*    *    *

Armitage's declaration might have ended the FBI investigation, but for two problems. First, that pesky 1x2x6 article sent the FBI looking for *six* leaks, leaks motivated by revenge rather than—as Armitage described his actions—by ignorance and gossip. Second, as the FBI interviewed administration officials, the stories didn't hold up. To really get to the bottom of the leak, it would have to pursue those unanswered questions.

Those two things were not, by themselves, fatal to the administration's efforts to put this affair behind it. After all, the only way to pursue the issue further would be to talk to journalists. And everyone in D.C. believed journalists would protect their sources. On October 5, 2003, in a cover story that would have its own ugly ironies before the case was done, *Time* magazine's

Michael Duffy, with contributions from Matt Cooper, Viveca Novak (no relation to Robert Novak), John Dickerson, and others, laid out the conventional wisdom clearly:

> There was President Bush at the University of Chicago, asking reporters who covered him to turn in anyone on his staff who had given up Plame. There was no danger of that, because any reporter who might have learned Plame's name in a leak is duty bound to shut up about it, even to federal investigators, if the situation comes to that.... The ultimate irony is that the administration may now be depending on journalists' rectitude.[137]

Two days later, on the same day that Novak first spoke to the FBI, President Bush agreed with *Time:*

> I mean this town is a—is a town full of people who like to leak information. And I don't know if we're going to find out the senior administration official. Now, this is a large administration, and there's a lot of senior officials. I don't have any idea. I'd like to. I want to know the truth. That's why I've instructed this staff of mine to cooperate fully with the investigators—full disclosure, everything we know the investigators will find out. I have no idea whether we'll find out who the leaker is—partially because, in all due respect to your profession, you do a very good job of protecting the leakers.[138]

On one thing, the journalists and the administration agreed: Journalists would not out their sources.

# CHAPTER 5

# BEAT THE PRESS

(January 2004–July 2005)

---

*While requiring [journalists] to testify may discourage future leaks,*
*discouraging leaks of this kind is precisely what the public interest requires.*
— Federal Judge David Tatel

From the time the Department of Justice announced that it would conduct
a criminal investigation into the leak of Valerie Wilson's CIA status, on
September 26, 2003, Democrats complained that the Bush administration
could not investigate itself in this case. They had good reason to complain.
The Department of Justice had conflicts of interest going all the way up the
chain of command from the FBI,[139] and Attorney General John Ashcroft,
one of those with a conflict, was getting briefings from the head of the
investigation.[140] After months of pressure, Ashcroft recused himself, and
on December 30, 2003, the newly appointed deputy attorney general,
James Comey, named Patrick Fitzgerald as special counsel to investigate
the leak.[141]

Fitzgerald was a stunning choice for a political appointee to make.
He had a reputation for taking on the worst kind of criminal—mobsters
and terrorists—and winning. While working in the U.S. Attorney's office in
Manhattan, Fitzgerald had won convictions of Sheikh Omar Abdel
Rahman, the spiritual leader of the World Trade Center bombers, and
Mafioso John Gambino. In 1998, he had indicted Public Enemy No. 1—
Osama bin Laden—on terrorism charges. Comey had chosen one of the
nation's toughest prosecutors to investigate the president and his top staff.

And Fitzgerald was not known for being swayed by political allegiance or influence. Fitzgerald's success in New York had attracted the attention of Senator Peter Fitzgerald (no relation), who was hoping to find a prosecutor incorruptible enough to clean up Chicago's legendary corruption. Patrick Fitzgerald was named U.S. Attorney for Northern Illinois in 2001, and he went after the graft in Chicago politics as determinedly as he had gone after terrorism and organized crime in New York. In one celebrated investigation, Fitzgerald methodically pursued corruption in the administration of the Republican governor, George Ryan, working his way up from illegally licensed truck drivers to indict Ryan, who as secretary of state had set up a system that gave them those licenses in exchange for bribes. Fitzgerald's team won at least seventy-five convictions in connection with the investigation, including Ryan's in 2006, making it one of the most successful investigations in Chicago history. Fitzgerald drew comparisons with Eliot Ness, the legendary prosecutor who took on Al Capone. Imagine a top Justice Department appointee picking Eliot Ness to investigate his own administration!

In all of his successes, Fitzgerald was noted for two things. First was his persistence, exhibited in cases like the Ryan investigation. Second was his creativity, his willingness to adopt novel approaches to pursue suspected criminals. For example, Fitzgerald used racketeering laws, which were designed to prosecute organized crime syndicates, to dismantle corrupt political machines like Ryan's and corrupt businesses like Conrad Black's media empire.[142] These characteristics came in handy while investigating the CIA leak case.

*   *   *

As special counsel on the case, Fitzgerald was tasked with learning the circumstances of all leaks of Valerie Wilson's identity, not just those to Robert Novak, and to determine whether any crimes had taken place, including any violations of the IIPA, which criminalizes the deliberate leaking of covert identities.[143] There were three known examples of potentially illegal leaks.[144] First was the leak *The Washington Post* admitted to having received on

July 12, 2003, which it had reported that October. Next were the sources for Robert Novak's July 14 column, which publicly exposed Wilson's identity. And finally there was the *Time* magazine story published July 17, which said, "Some government officials have noted to *Time* in interviews…that Wilson's wife, Valerie Plame, is a CIA official who monitors the proliferation of weapons of mass destruction."[145]

When Fitzgerald took over the case, he received the files from forty FBI interviews conducted in the preceding months, including interviews with Richard Armitage, the deputy secretary of state; I. Lewis "Scooter" Libby, Vice President Cheney's chief of staff; White House strategist Karl Rove; Novak; Joe and Valerie Plame Wilson; and aides involved in press contacts at the time of the leak. Fitzgerald also had administration phone logs covering many of the calls made in early July. Supposedly, he had all notes and e-mails relating to the allegations that Iraq had bought uranium from Niger.[146]

Fitzgerald began, then, with some idea of which journalists had received the three leaks and of what administration officials had said in their statements to investigators. But one of the big questions Fitzgerald had to answer pertained to Libby's FBI testimony. As the defender of Dick Cheney's views publicly, Libby was right at the center of the controversy because of the way Wilson's column implicated the Office of the Vice President.

Fitzgerald had the reports from two FBI interviews of Libby, one from October 14 and another from November 26. In those interviews, Libby had explained that he learned on July 10 or 11, in a conversation with NBC's Tim Russert, that Valerie Wilson worked at the CIA:

> So then he said—I said—he said, sorry—he, Mr. Russert, said to me, did you know that Ambassador Wilson's wife, or his wife, works at the CIA? And I said, no, I don't know that. And then he said, yeah—yes, all the reporters know it. And I said, again, I don't know that. I just wanted to be clear that I wasn't confirming anything for him on this.[147]

Libby told the FBI that on July 12 he passed on this information to Matthew Cooper of *Time,* Judith Miller of *The New York Times,* and a third reporter,

possibly Glenn Kessler of *The Washington Post*.[148] But Libby claimed to
have told the journalists that he wasn't sure whether the information about
Valerie Wilson was true.[149] In short, Libby was admitting he had passed the
information to some journalists, but claimed to have learned of Valerie
Wilson's identity from journalists. If that was true, Libby could not be held
criminally liable for the leaking of classified information under the IIPA.

But Fitzgerald—and the FBI investigators before him—also had Libby's
notes from the time period, and there they found something suspicious.[150]
They discovered that Libby had a note about Valerie Wilson on June 12—
almost a month before he said he first learned about her from his conversation with Russert. The note recorded that Cheney had informed Libby
that Joseph Wilson's wife worked in the Counterproliferation Division
(CPD) of the CIA. This would mean Libby had learned of Wilson's identity via classified channels rather than gossip from reporters, making any
leak of her identity a potential IIPA violation.

Libby had an excuse, of course. He told FBI investigators that he had
simply forgotten that Cheney had told him about Valerie Wilson, and so
learned it again from Russert "as if it were new." It was an awfully suspicious
story, one that seemed clumsily designed to disconnect the eventual leaks
from a great deal of deliberate information-gathering about the Wilsons on
the part of the vice president's office a month earlier. But in order to nail
down the truth, Fitzgerald needed to hear directly from the journalists
about what they were leaked and when.

So Fitzgerald decided to do what everyone in Washington swore
couldn't be done: Get journalists to talk about conversations with confidential sources. On January 2, just days after his appointment, Fitzgerald asked
administration officials to sign waivers allowing reporters to speak to investigators about their conversations with the officials regarding Joe and
Valerie Wilson.[151] Most observers and political pundits dismissed this tactic
as an attempt to appear thorough and suggested that the waivers would
be regarded as coerced. But administration officials signed the waivers,
preserving the appearance that the White House was cooperating fully with
the investigation.

With the waivers in hand, Fitzgerald started by pursuing the testimony of Bob Novak, the one known recipient of the leak, in the first weeks of January. In April, after some administration officials had testified before the grand jury and questions about the stories remained, Fitzgerald pursued the other journalists most likely to have received identified leaks and requested testimony from Russert to determine whether Libby had told the truth about their conversation.

Fitzgerald realized he was doing something momentous. Journalists considered their sources and their conversations with them to be sacrosanct. So he approached the issue cautiously. He didn't ask them to reveal their sources;[152] rather, he figured out who the sources were by using phone records and other documents turned over by the administration. Then he approached journalists with waivers from their sources, asking only for a description of what had transpired in the conversations. The waivers released the journalists from any promises about confidentiality they had made; the phone records allowed Fitzgerald to name the sources himself, rather than asking the journalists to reveal them. And in several cases, Fitzgerald's approach worked.

One of them was *The Washington Post*, where, in April, Fitzgerald pursued the testimony of Glenn Kessler and Walter Pincus. Kessler, who hadn't spoken to Libby about the Wilsons at all, revealed that he wasn't the recipient of the Wilson leak. At that point, Fitzgerald knew that Pincus almost certainly was, so he subpoenaed Pincus. Pincus fought the subpoena, but when he discovered the administration official had admitted he was Pincus's source, Pincus went ahead and testified. Neither Kessler nor Pincus had to reveal his source's identity to Fitzgerald.

Fitzgerald's strategy also worked with Novak. Novak fretted he would have to accept the waivers from—and testify about—anyone who might be his source:

> The problem facing me was that the special prosecutor had obtained signed waivers from every official who might have given me information about Wilson's wife.[153]

When Fitzgerald informed Novak that he had waivers from his three sources, Novak agreed to be interviewed about those three sources. Unlike Pincus and Kessler, Novak didn't even contact his sources to get a personalized waiver. Fitzgerald was able to reconstruct Novak's version of his conversations without forcing Novak to reveal the names of his sources.

But there was one problem that Fitzgerald had not anticipated. By agreeing to limit the journalists' testimony to their conversations with the sources he knew about, Fitzgerald risked the loss of testimony regarding sources he *didn't* know about. This is what happened with *Time*'s Matt Cooper, who had just been assigned to cover the White House a few weeks before the Niger controversy erupted, and in that role had teamed up on stories cataloging the way the administration attacked Wilson in response to his op-ed in the *Times*. At first, Fitzgerald subpoenaed Cooper generally, and after Cooper's attempt to quash the subpoena failed, he was charged with contempt. Then Fitzgerald offered to limit his questions to a conversation Cooper had had with Libby on July 12. Fitzgerald hoped to confirm or rebut Libby's story that he had simply passed on Valerie Wilson's identity to Cooper, downplaying the leak by claiming he was just passing on news he had learned from other journalists.

On August 22, 2004, the night before his sentencing on contempt charges, Cooper called Libby to ask for a waiver to testify:

> The lawyers representing Time Inc. and me, who supported my making that call, thought Libby might well do so. After all, he had granted a waiver to a *Washington Post* reporter, and Tim Russert of NBC had just avoided contempt by testifying about his end of his conversation with Libby. Most important, my exchange with Libby about Wilson had been short and, in my thinking and Time Inc.'s, not especially provocative.[154]

Cooper knew that if he asked for a waiver, Libby would be under some pressure to grant it, since refusing to do so would make it look as if Libby was not cooperating. But since, according to Cooper's own judgment, his conversation with Libby was not that incriminating, he figured he could go ahead and ask with no risk of forcing Libby to give the waiver.[155] Cooper didn't wait for an invitation—he called and asked for a waiver, and Libby granted it.

The next day Cooper gave a deposition about his July 12, 2003, conversation with Libby. Cooper said that in the middle of a discussion about the Niger allegations, he brought up Valerie Wilson himself:

> Basically, I asked Libby if he had heard anything about Wilson's wife having been involved in sending him to Niger. Libby responded with words to the effect of, "Yeah, I've heard that too."[156]

Cooper's testimony revealed something unexpected. If Libby had only confirmed Valerie Wilson's identity, it meant Cooper had *another source* who had given him her identity in the first place. But since Fitzgerald had agreed to limit Cooper's testimony to his conversation with Libby, he couldn't ask Cooper about the other source.[157]

Fitzgerald also ran into another problem: Journalists trying to protect their relationships rather than their reporting. In Russert's case, for instance, Fitzgerald wanted to find out whether Libby had testified truthfully when he said that Russert had told him about Valerie Wilson's identity in July. Libby had called Russert—who is senior vice president of NBC News and the network's Washington, D.C., bureau chief—to complain that MSNBC talk show host Chris Matthews had attributed the inclusion of the Niger allegations in the State of the Union speech to Cheney and Libby.[158] So Fitzgerald was asking about a conversation that Russert had had in his role as a manager, not a reporter, and he was asking what Russert had told Libby, not vice versa. Given the context of Libby's phone call, it was not a journalist-source conversation at all, and Russert was not being asked to reveal a source or what the source said.

But that's not how Russert saw it. Russert simply claimed that *every* conversation he had—whether a source was speaking on background or not, whether he was collecting or passing on news—should be protected.

A conversation between a prominent journalist and a senior government official cannot be artificially parsed or surgically removed from the realities of newsgathering, as the Special Prosecutor apparently contends.... And there is no basis for the Special Prosecutor's suggestion that the purpose for which a source contacts a journalist somehow governs whether their subsequent communications implicate the news gathering function. To the contrary, the full-time occupation of a journalist such as Mr. Russert is to uncover newsworthy information from his sources, whether he encounters them in a formal interview, at a cocktail reception, or in a phone call initiated by one of them to complain about news coverage.[159]

There's a quip among bloggers to describe journalists who have been compromised by their desire to retain access to the powerful: They've traded reporting for cocktail weenies. When source protection extends to every single conversation a journalist has, whether on or off the job, it serves to protect the journalist's status within the power elite, rather than the journalist's ability to do their job of reporting the truth and holding the powerful accountable. And it makes it a lot more likely that the powerful will hide behind journalists as they spread unsubstantiated dirt.

Russert wasn't the only journalist extending source protection to everyone he spoke with; Novak was doing some of the same. Of Armitage, he said "you just know" this kind of conversation is on background. And his conversations with Rove were generally not for attribution.[160] Effectively, Novak had protected all of his conversations with almost everyone in his life, regardless of any specific promise of confidentiality.

In dealing with journalists, Fitzgerald also ran into some, like Judith Miller of the *Times,* who treated waivers as contingent based on how much damage their testimony could do to their source. Miller had never published a story on the Wilsons, though she claims she pitched the story to her editors.[161] But Fitzgerald subpoenaed her after he got Russert's testimony, on August 12 and 14, 2004.

Fitzgerald needed Miller's testimony for several reasons. Libby had testified that he spoke with Miller twice during the week of July 7—on July 8 and July 12.[162] Libby had testified that Valerie Wilson wasn't the focus of his July 8 meeting with Miller. But since Libby's story about getting the name from Russert now appeared to be untrue, it seemed likely that Libby was hiding something about his meeting with Miller. Perhaps Libby had told Miller of Valerie Wilson's identity, which might mean he had violated the IIPA. Or, as many speculated at the time, perhaps *Miller* had told *Libby* of Wilson's identity, in which case there would be merit to Libby's claim he had heard of Valerie Wilson's identity from a journalist after all. In any case, Fitzgerald needed Miller's testimony before he could determine whether Libby was guilty of a crime.

When Miller got her subpoena, in the fall of 2004, she had Floyd Abrams, the *Time*'s lawyer, contact Libby's lawyer, Joseph Tate, to inquire about a waiver from Libby. According to Abrams, Tate freed Miller to speak—but he added a detail that made Miller hesitate. Libby, Tate said, had testified that he had not told Miller of Valerie Wilson's identity, and certainly not her covert status or name. The problem was, Miller had both the names "Valerie Flame" and "Victoria Wilson" in her notes of their meeting. "Did the references in her notes to 'Valerie Flame' and 'Victoria Wilson' suggest that she would have to contradict Mr. Libby's account of their conversations?"[163] Miller wondered.

Miller believed that Tate was sending her a message: If she couldn't corroborate Libby's testimony, she should not testify. "Judy believed Libby was afraid of her testimony," the *Times* reported Executive Editor Bill Keller saying. "She thought Libby had reason to be afraid of her testimony."[164] Abrams even claims that Tate explicitly warned him against Miller testifying. Tate disputes that he gave specific warnings, but he doesn't dispute that he told Abrams how Libby had testified, a remarkable move. This was enough to demonstrate to Miller that truthful testimony would imperil Libby.[165] She therefore considered the waiver to be coerced. So, in spite of the fact that Tate had given Miller the same waiver he gave three other journalists, Miller sat on that waiver and refused to testify.

After that failed negotiation, the *Times* turned Miller into a First Amendment martyr. Miller's role as a martyr for source protection is an odd one, given that in a story she wrote in April 2003, Miller *had* exposed a source.[166] Shortly after the article had appeared, the *Times* had issued a correction and an apology. But in October 2004, the newspaper went on the offensive, publishing an editorial that decried Fitzgerald's attempts to get Miller to testify:

> A prosecutor's investigation into an apparent attempt by the Bush administration to punish a political opponent by revealing classified information has veered terribly off course. It threatens grievous harm to freedom of the press and the vital protection it provides against government misconduct.[167]

The same editorial hailing the importance of protecting sources went on to explain why Miller was refusing to testify: "Ms. Miller declined to testify, or to seek a waiver, on the basis that any consent Mr. Libby granted under a threat of firing could not be considered truly voluntary." The statement misrepresented several things. It claimed that Miller didn't seek a waiver, though in fact she had initiated conversations to do so. It said Miller believed the waiver to be coerced because Libby signed it under threat of firing, but it failed to mention her belief that her testimony would incriminate Libby. Most stunning was the editorial's mention of Libby's name—even though Libby was not publicly known to be Miller's source at this time! While preaching the need to protect sources, this editorial effectively revealed one.

And then the *Times* made a curious claim: "The specter of reporters' being imprisoned merely for doing their jobs is something that should worry everyone who cherishes the First Amendment and the essential role of a free press in a democracy."

But the job the *Times* claimed to be protecting involved, in this case, the propagation of a smear. And therein lies the real problem with the attacks on Fitzgerald in his pursuit of journalists who were leaked information about Valerie Wilson's identity. In all the chest-thumping about the First

Amendment and "source protection" and journalists simply "doing their jobs," the very reason for enshrining journalistic privilege got lost. The reporter's privilege of confidentiality is designed to protect those who provide journalists with information of importance to the American public. The idea is to allow whistleblowers to reveal information about corruption or danger or lies without the threat of losing their job.

But in this case, the leaks were made by the powerful—top White House officials—and they were made as retribution, not in any public interest. And they were made in retribution for *precisely the kind of activity the reporter's privilege is supposed to protect:* someone coming forward with information about mistakes or misjudgments made by the government. Effectively, this situation flipped the First Amendment on its head. Truly powerful people were using journalists as shields to launch attacks on a critic.

Several of the journalists involved in this case—Russert, Miller, Novak, even Bob Woodward—have made legendary careers by cultivating the favor of the powerful, who in turn feed them exclusive leaks or interviews usually designed to advance a political agenda. In such a world, it becomes hard to distinguish whether a journalist is protecting a source in order to promote the circulation of important news or to protect their access to the powerful, and with it their own prestige. Ultimately, it's as much about protecting one's access to cocktail weenies as it is about protecting free speech.

* * *

Fitzgerald slowly began to uncover pieces of evidence that illuminated the questions he set out to answer: Who had leaked Valerie Wilson's identity and why had they leaked it? But his limited approach also limited his findings.

Fitzgerald obtained the testimony of Walter Pincus, the recipient of the *Washington Post* leak, who later described his testimony thus:

On July 12, 2003, an administration official, who was talking to me confidentially about a matter involving alleged Iraqi nuclear activities, veered off the precise matter we were discussing and told me that the White House had not paid attention to former Ambassador Joseph Wilson's CIA-sponsored February 2002 trip to Niger because it was set up as a boondoggle by his wife, an analyst with the agency working on weapons of mass destruction.

I didn't write about that information at that time because I did not believe it true that she had arranged his Niger trip.[168]

Pincus's source has not been revealed publicly. But we can assume Fitzgerald determined Pincus's source had not violated the IIPA statute, since the source had not revealed that Valerie Wilson was covert.

And by obtaining Novak's testimony, Fitzgerald got an explanation—albeit a dubious one—for the source of Novak's leak. Novak testified on January 14, 2004, that Richard Armitage was his first source and Karl Rove his confirming source. Novak's testimony differed from Armitage's on the issue of how Armitage had described Valerie Wilson's role at the CIA and how intentional the leak seemed. Until he clarified the discrepancies in that story, Fitzgerald couldn't charge an IIPA violation.

But in his pursuit of the *Time* magazine leak, Fitzgerald's novel approach broke down. When Cooper testified that Libby was just his confirming source, not his original source, it gave Fitzgerald further evidence that Libby had lied to him. Indeed, it suggested that Libby, by implying he was the original source for Cooper, may have covered up someone else's involvement. But Fitzgerald, it appears, did not know who Cooper's source was; there were no phone records in the White House logs, nor any other evidence, that pointed toward a potential source. Having agreed to limit Cooper's questioning to his conversation with Libby, Fitzgerald remained blind to another—Cooper's most important—source.

And this might be true of anyone. Fitzgerald's willingness to limit questioning to what he already knew gave him blind spots. By restricting his investigation to known leak recipients, Fitzgerald may have missed leaks to journalists who didn't publish a story.[169] By having journalists testify only about discussions during the week of the leak, Fitzgerald may have missed critical conversations that happened *before* Wilson published his *Times* op-ed.[170] By questioning the journalists only about identified sources, he risked missing key information provided by earlier sources.[171]

And there was one more potential problem with Fitzgerald's approach—the possibility that a journalist would simply refuse to testify.

Judith Miller did just that. On July 6, 2005, Chief Judge Thomas Hogan of the federal district court in Washington, D.C., jailed Miller for contempt of court. In a blizzard of cameras, federal marshals led Miller away to the same jail where Zacarias Moussaoui, the terrorist tied to the 9/11 attack, was imprisoned.

When Miller went to jail rather than testify about her source, Fitzgerald's approach seemed to many to have been an utter failure. Maybe Miller was deliberately protecting an ideological ally. Maybe her source was simply using the dependable structure of source protection as a convenient hiding place. At the very least, however, Fitzgerald had jailed the wrong person—the one who *received* the leak rather than the one who maliciously passed it on. As Joe Wilson commented on Miller's jailing, "Ms. Miller joined my wife, Valerie, and her twenty years of service to this nation as collateral damage" in the attack on him.[172]

With Miller going to jail in July 2005, Fitzgerald was not much closer to his goal than he was when he had started, eighteen months earlier. In October 2003, a *Time* magazine article had predicted that "there was no danger of [of reporters turning in their sources] because any reporter who might have learned Plame's name in a leak is duty bound to shut up about it." Matthew Cooper, now clearly at the center of the leak investigation, had contributed to that article. From their safe anonymity, the White House officials who leaked Valerie Plame Wilson's identity probably took great comfort in *Time*'s predictions.

# CHAPTER 6

# THE SPIN DOCTOR

(September 2003–August 2006)

---

*BOB WOODWARD: And you know what? The special prosecutor, Fitzgerald, in a way, has discovered that there is an underground railroad of information in Washington. You're smiling because no one knows more about it than you.*

*CARL BERNSTEIN: Well, you were down there.*

*WOODWARD: Well, you talk to people, you talk to somebody in the White House or the CIA or the Democratic Party, and you say, "I've heard or I understand; what are you hearing?" And one of the discoveries in all of this is that reporters, in asking questions, convey information to even somebody like Karl Rove.*

— *Meet the Press*, NBC, July 17, 2005

When Valerie Plame Wilson's identity was leaked as retaliation for her husband's criticism of the Bush administration, the obvious suspect was Karl Rove. The ugly details, the anonymous sources, the Machiavellian machinations, all reeked of Rove's modus operandi.

After all, Rove (who is often called Bush's Brain) had, at various points in his career, used similar tactics to effectively create George W. Bush as a political phenomenon. The two first met in 1973, when Rove was a special assistant to Bush's father, George H. W. Bush, who then headed the Republican National Committee (RNC). Rove saw in the son's cowboy boots, charisma, and swagger the makings of a great political candidate. Rove went on to work as a Texas-based political consultant, providing direct mail consulting and campaign management for a number of Republicans.

Along the way, he acquired a reputation for having a mastery of details, obsessive planning, deep study of electoral politics—and underhanded tactics. Rove contributed greatly to turning the formerly reliable Democratic stronghold of Texas into a staunchly Republican state, and he was determined to replicate this success on a national scale, building a permanent Republican majority. And he was going to do so with Bush as his candidate.

Rove worked on George W. Bush's unsuccessful congressional campaign in 1978, and in 1990 encouraged him to run for governor of Texas (Bush decided against it). When Bush did run, in 1994, against incumbent governor Ann Richards, Rove used some of his famous attack tactics, mobilizing Christian conservatives through gay-baiting. For example, as a way of puncturing Richards's good record of diversity in hiring, Rove insinuated that her administration was hiring unqualified lesbians.

During Bush's presidential bid in 2000, Rove's methods got even uglier. After Senator John McCain's surprise victory in the Republican primary in New Hampshire, Rove set out to win the South Carolina primary at all costs. A secretive group funded by rich Texans started conducting nasty "push polls," suggesting to voters that McCain had a black child (in fact, he and his wife had adopted a Bangladeshi child) and that McCain's wife, Cindy, had drug problems. In 2004, another group, financed by some of the same rich Texans, alleged that Senator John Kerry lied about how he got wounded in Vietnam. Key to most of Rove's attacks was a mastery of the press and the ability to leak scandalous allegations anonymously—usually playing on perception rather than fact—to friendly reporters.

When the retaliatory leak against Joe Wilson surfaced in 2003, observers saw Rove's fingerprints all over it. Wilson more or less accused Rove of masterminding the smear; on August 21, 2003, he said, "It's of keen interest to me to see whether or not we can get Karl Rove frog-marched out of the White House in handcuffs."[173] Wilson had good reason to think Rove was involved. As Wilson revealed to journalists, Rove had called MSNBC's Chris Matthews shortly after the leak and said that Wilson's wife was "fair game." Clearly, Rove was a key player in the "game" of smearing Joe Wilson.

Because Rove was the leading suspect, and because he was absolutely indispensable, the September 2003 announcement of the investigation posed a real challenge for the White House. While the administration wanted to find a way to appear to be cooperating, it needed to protect Rove. During a briefing on September 29, spokesperson Scott McClellan assured journalists that "if anyone in this administration was involved in it, they would no longer be in this administration." McClellan went on to say that any mention of Rove's involvement was "a ridiculous suggestion,"[174] but he backed off from making any such categorical denial about Scooter Libby, the chief of staff for Vice President Cheney.[175]

Rove hired a lawyer, Robert Luskin, who would complement his strengths. As a flashy Democrat, Luskin might seem an odd match for the hyperpartisan Rove.[176] Yet Luskin, a former journalist, sowed disinformation among the press corps, repeatedly parsing the truth.[177] And a long series of anonymous leaks from "lawyers involved in the case" provided tips to journalists that directed their focus in ways that suited Rove's legal and PR strategies.

Luskin was kept busy. Sometime before October 27, 2003, Rove was interviewed by the FBI.[178] He then appeared before the grand jury five times: twice in February 2004, once on October 15, 2004, once on October 14, 2005, and once on April 26, 2006. Clearly, Rove had a deep involvement in the CIA leak case. So far, however, Rove has managed to escape both legal charges and any political penalty, such as the loss of his influential job at the White House. He has done so by using the same tactics he mastered during his political career—surreptitious power plays and manipulation of journalists eager to retain access to the White House.

\* \* \*

Rove's involvement passed largely unnoticed after the initial days of excitement surrounding the investigation. His first two grand jury appearances went unreported. And even though he testified in October 2004, just two days after Matt Cooper's attempts to quash a second subpoena were denied, no one made any connection between the two events.[179]

But Rove's low profile changed in July 2005, after Cooper's appeals of the subpoena failed and the judge overseeing the grand jury gave *Time* and Cooper (along with Judith Miller) one week to comply with subpoenas. On July 1, MSNBC political analyst and *West Wing* producer Lawrence O'Donnell revealed that Rove was Cooper's source.[180] The next day, Rove favorite Michael Isikoff of *Newsweek* reported that Luskin admitted that Cooper had interviewed Rove for his article, but that Rove "never knowingly disclosed classified information" and "did not tell any reporter that Valerie Plame worked for the CIA."[181] The day before Cooper testified, reliable conservative mouthpiece Byron York published an article repeating Luskin's accusation that Cooper had "burned" Rove, sending a signal that Rove's version of their conversation differed from Cooper's.[182] And in a *Wall Street Journal* article on July 6, the day Cooper would set off to jail, Luskin said, "If Matt Cooper is going to jail to protect a source, it's not Karl he's protecting."[183]

That line prompted Cooper to do something he had done unprompted with Libby: seek a personal waiver from Rove to testify. Cooper's lawyer, Richard Sauber, later explained his response to that line: "I took that as an invitation to pick up the phone and say if that really is the case, give us a personal and direct waiver so that Matt can testify."[184] On July 13, Matt Cooper testified before the grand jury. Cooper would publish an account of his testimony on July 16, describing the whole conversation with Rove as steeped in secrecy. "Don't get too far out on Wilson," Rove advised Cooper.[185] Cooper revealed that Rove offered up the information that Valerie Wilson worked at the CIA. Rove also told Cooper that some things would be declassified shortly that would cast doubt on his report. "I've already said too much," Rove said as he hung up.

Spurred by the revelation that Rove had talked to Cooper about Valerie Plame Wilson, ninety-one Democratic congressmen sent a letter to George Bush on July 14, quoting his own professions of concern about the leak and demanding either an explanation or a resignation from Rove. Bush would soon backtrack from earlier promises to fire anyone involved in the leak, promising this time merely that "if someone committed a crime, they will no longer work in my administration."[186]

On July 15, *The New York Times* published a front-page article that quoted Luskin reporting that Rove was Novak's second source.[187] After nearly two years of denying any involvement in the leak, Rove was now tied to two of the three known leaks to reporters.

* * *

That's when the distraction campaign began. Rove needed to get the spotlight off himself and onto someone else. That someone turned out to be former White House press secretary Ari Fleischer. On the same day that the *Times* identified Rove as one of Novak's two sources, the New York *Daily News* published an article citing unnamed sources "close to the probe" explaining that, in addition to Rove, the grand jury was investigating Fleischer's role in the Plame affair. "Ari's name keeps popping up," one source told the paper.[188]

Clearly, the behind-the-scenes media campaign was giving reporters fresh meat (in the form of Fleischer) to distract them from Rove. The campaign based its insinuations about Fleischer's involvement on what is now called the INR memo, the same document from which Armitage had learned of Valerie Wilson's identity. The memo was faxed to Air Force One during President Bush's trip to Africa during the week of July 6, 2003. The *Daily News* story, quoting the unnamed sources, pointed out that the memo "included background on Wilson" and that it "appears to be a key" to revealing who gave Valerie Plame Wilson's name to Robert Novak.

A whole slew of stories in the national media followed in quick succession, each of them describing the memo and Fleischer's purported incrimination due to it.[189] The press, which just a day before had been in a frenzy reporting Rove's demonstrable role in the CIA leak, had abruptly shifted its attention to chasing down a story implicating Fleischer and (to a lesser degree) Colin Powell in unsubstantiated ways.

One typical and egregious example of such misdirection was a Bloomberg story that began with a relevant question: "What did [Rove] know and when did he know it?" But then it answered that question by pointing to Fleischer:

On the same day the memo was prepared [July 7], White House phone logs show Novak placed a call to White House Press Secretary Ari Fleischer, according to lawyers familiar with the case and a witness who has testified before the grand jury. Those people say it is not clear whether Fleischer returned the call, and Fleischer has refused to comment.

The Novak call may loom large in the investigation because Fleischer was among a group of administration officials who left Washington later that day on a presidential trip to Africa. On the flight to Africa, Fleischer was seen perusing the State Department memo on Wilson and his wife, according to a former administration official who was also on the trip.

In addition, on July 8, 2003, the day after the memo was sent, Novak discussed Wilson and his wife with Rove, who had remained in Washington, according to the New York Times.[190]

The story suggested the following scenario: Fleischer looked at the INR memo, learned of Valerie Wilson's purported role in Wilson's trip, returned the call to Novak, and passed on the information about Valerie Wilson, and then Novak brought it up with Rove. Barely noticed among the flurry of articles was a denial: "Fleischer told the grand jury that he never saw the memo, a person familiar with [his] testimony said, speaking on condition of anonymity.... Fleischer has told the grand jury that he did not return Novak's call, a person familiar with the testimony said."[191]

Furthermore, the INR memo simply could not have prepared Fleischer to leak to Novak. Two articles pointed out that the memo didn't include the name, Plame, used in Novak's column,[192] and two others noted that the memo didn't identify Valerie Wilson as covert.[193] (Indeed, an Isikoff article published the year before had pointed out both of these facts.)[194] And yet many reporters continued to focus on Fleischer, such as Jim VandeHei of *The Washington Post*, who kept reporting the Fleischer story until October 2005, even after co-authoring a July 2005 article that made clear the memo couldn't be the source of the Novak leak.[195]

We now know the insinuation doesn't make any sense. Fleischer testified that Libby told him on July 7, before the memo was sent, "The Vice-President did not send Ambassador Wilson to Niger...the CIA sent Ambassador Wilson to Niger...[H]e was sent by his wife...[S]he works in...the Counterproliferation area of the CIA." Libby also made sure Fleischer knew this was sensitive, calling it "hush hush," "it's on the QT."[196] It's possible that Fleischer did leak Valerie Wilson's involvement to a reporter. But when, on July 11, he pushed John Dickerson of *Time* magazine and other journalists to look into the roots of the trip, sending them to discover Valerie Wilson's purported involvement themselves, he stopped short of leaking her classified identity. And according to Fleischer, the provenance of any information he leaked didn't come from the INR memo, it came from Libby.

The timing of leaks about the INR memo—particularly in relation to Fleischer—makes sense only in the context of the revelations about Rove and the more distant threat of Miller's testimony. While some of the articles in July 2005 suggested that witnesses had recently been asked about Fleischer's role, the bulk of interviews with administration officials took place in early 2004, with a second batch after the Senate released its report on Iraq intelligence in July 2004. And one article makes clear that the questions about the INR memo came much earlier in the investigation.[197] Yet all of a sudden, just as scrutiny turned to Rove, the series of articles focusing on Fleischer appeared.

The leak campaign against Fleischer served one other purpose, albeit a crafty one. Since Libby had told Fleischer of Valerie Wilson's identity in such a way as to make it appear that Libby knew her identity was classified, Fleischer was a potential witness against Libby. Focusing suspicion on Fleischer would undermine his value as a witness if Libby were to face charges.[198]

The leaks about Fleischer and the INR memo served several purposes. They distracted the press corps from validated revelations of Rove's involvement; they provided an alternative source for the Novak leak and a provenance for that leak *outside* the White House; and they impugned a potential witness at a trial. All of this was possible because some journalists didn't question what they were being fed by their unnamed sources.

*   *   *

By the fall of 2005, the pressure started to build on the White House. The grand jury Patrick Fitzgerald used to investigate the CIA leak case was due to expire on October 28, placing an artificial deadline on his work. He had to either bring charges by then or convene a new grand jury. For political reasons, he would need new evidence of a crime in order to convene a new grand jury. Failing that, he would have to end the investigation.

Observers speculated about who might be indicted, and Fleischer, Libby, and Rove were the common suspects. Judith Miller had testified on September 30 and on October 12; her account of her testimony focused closely on Libby, though she also mentioned she had been asked directly about Dick Cheney's role. Miller did not mention Rove at all. As the grand jury's expiration date approached, a flurry of news reports appeared about the confusion and panic within the White House, which had no idea which—or how many—of its key players would be indicted.

In the middle of that panic, Rove testified before the grand jury, his fourth appearance. Clearly, Fitzgerald had Rove in his sights. Rove was walking a dangerous line in his testimony about Cooper. In his first two appearances before the grand jury, in February 2004, Rove had made no mention of talking with Cooper. He had only mentioned it in October 2004, when it seemed likely Cooper would be forced to testify. Unless Rove had a good explanation for changing his story, he faced a perjury charge.

At this time, the role of Deputy Secretary of State Richard Armitage in the leak was known only to investigators. Novak's revised story claimed that Rove had served only as his confirming source, while Armitage was his main source. Though Armitage testified that he hadn't mentioned Valerie Wilson's role in the CIA's counterproliferation division (CPD), much less her covert status, Novak said he had described her as being in CPD. So long as Armitage retained the credibility he won by coming forward willingly and without a lawyer, the conflict reflected badly on Rove, because it suggested that, as Novak's other source, he had leaked that information to Novak.

At that moment, amid the flurry of speculation about indictments, there was a set of leaks similar to those impugning Fleischer—this time pointing to a "Mr. X" as Novak's source. A leak to Viveca Novak (no relation to Robert Novak) and Mike Allen of *Time* magazine on October 17—attributed to "a source close to Rove" and a "lawyer who's involved in the case"—provided a clue to Mr. X's identity:

> But Fitzgerald's intentions aren't the only mystery. Another character in the drama remains unnamed: the original source for columnist Robert Novak, who wrote the first piece naming Plame. Fitzgerald, says a lawyer who's involved in the case, "knows who it is—and it's not someone at the White House."[199]

Apparently, these same sources thought that Bob Woodward might know Mr. X's identity, and could be pressured into revealing it. On October 27, on CNN's *Larry King Live*, Isikoff pushed Woodward to cough it up:

> ISIKOFF: I talked to a source at the White House late this afternoon who told me that Bob is going to have a bombshell in tomorrow's paper identifying the Mr. X source who is behind the whole thing. So, I don't know, maybe this is Bob's opportunity.
>
> KING: Come clean.
>
> WOODWARD: I wish I did have a bombshell. I don't even have a firecracker. I'm sorry. In fact, I mean this tells you something about the atmosphere here. I got a call from somebody in the CIA saying he got a call from the best *New York Times* reporter on this saying exactly that I supposedly had a bombshell.... Finally, this went around that I was going to do it tonight or in the paper. Finally, Len Downie, who is the editor of *The Washington Post,* called me and said, "I hear you have a bombshell. Would you let me in on it?"[200]

Someone, clearly, wanted the identity of Mr. X—and that he didn't work at the White House—revealed, and they were willing to use journalists to force it out.[201]

The next day, October 28, Karl Rove got a reprieve. Fitzgerald unveiled a five-count indictment of Libby, but he had no indictment for Rove. To be sure, Rove was recognizably listed in Libby's indictment as "Official A," often used to identify a co-conspirator who may soon be indicted in a crime. And Fitzgerald pointedly said he would use a standing grand jury for further matters, promising, "I will not end the investigation until I can look anyone in the eye and tell them that we have carried out our responsibility sufficiently to be sure that we've done what we could to make intelligent decisions about when to end the investigation." But for the moment, at least, Rove's efforts to escape indictment had succeeded. And in the months following Libby's indictment, Rove's ongoing strategy for avoiding an indictment became clear: He kept tossing out details that didn't exactly explain away his own actions, but did make it harder for Fitzgerald to charge him for those actions.

And then, on November 14, 2005, Bob Woodward finally revealed his bombshell— only it wasn't exactly what Isikoff had in mind. Woodward said he had been leaked Valerie Wilson's identity in mid-June 2003. When Woodward saw Libby's indictment, and saw that Fitzgerald dated the first leak to June 23, he pushed his source to come forward.[202] Shortly thereafter, Woodward's source and Woodward would both testify about that earlier leak.

The one detail Woodward had left out—Mr. X's identity—wouldn't be known until several months later (though it was leaked widely among conservative pundits). But we now know the story. At a meeting in mid-June 2003 with his friend Armitage, Woodward had boasted that he knew the identity of the envoy to Niger who had appeared in the story his *Post* colleague, Walter Pincus, had published the day before: Joe Wilson.[203] As if in a contest over who had the best gossip, Armitage responded that he knew that "Wilson's wife worked for the CIA on weapons of mass destruction as a WMD analyst."[204] And of course Armitage was the same Mr. X that was Novak's first source.

Woodward didn't reveal the identity of Mr. X publicly, as Isikoff had pushed him to do. But his bombshell may have had the desired effect anyway. Before Woodward convinced Armitage to go forward, Fitzgerald had heard two stories about the Novak leak, one from someone (Armitage) who had come forward of his own accord and the other from someone (Novak) who had noticeably changed his story. But now Armitage had to admit that he had forgotten telling a journalist about Valerie Wilson's identity.[205] That would make it hard to use Armitage as a witness in any trial attempting to prove that Rove's claims to have forgotten leaks to journalists were false. And it would lessen Armitage's credibility about the Novak leak. After the pressure on Woodward led him to reveal his earlier leak, one of Rove's main legal concerns diminished.

Woodward's revelation also highlighted once again the shortcoming in Fitzgerald's approach. As it had with Matt Cooper, Fitzgerald's willingness to limit testimony to identifiable conversations with known leak recipients effectively shielded the conversation between Armitage and Woodward from view. While some journalists criticized Fitzgerald for not finding out earlier about Woodward's conversation—and not issuing a subpoena to Woodward—the same journalists would have been up in arms had Fitzgerald gone after *all* journalists who had contact with White House officials during the weeks or months before the leak surfaced in Novak's column. It was Fitzgerald's deference to reporters that made him take a limited approach of only calling on known leak recipients in the media, rather than casting a wider fishing net in hopes of coming up with something significant.

Woodward's bombshell relieved one of Rove's concerns. But he had another. He needed to explain why he came forward and admitted to a conversation with Cooper just when it became clear that Cooper would have to testify. Otherwise, he might be indicted for lying about not remembering that conversation in his first two grand jury appearances in February 2004. When Rove testified in October 2004, he offered up an e-mail he wrote to Stephen Hadley just after speaking to Cooper on July 11, 2003, by way of explanation:[206]

Matt Cooper called to give me a heads-up that he's got a welfare reform story coming. When he finished his brief heads-up he immediately launched into Niger. Isn't this damaging? Hasn't the president been hurt? I didn't take the bait, but I said if I were him I wouldn't get *Time* far out in front on this.[207]

He testified that he found the e-mail, remembered the conversation, and so came forward to testify. But the e-mail by itself wouldn't remove the risk of a perjury indictment. Rove had to answer why he had found the e-mail in October 2004 rather than October 2003, when such materials were subpoenaed. And Rove needed to explain why he had looked for it at all, since he claimed not to remember the Cooper conversation. To answer that question, just before the indictment, Rove's lawyer, Robert Luskin, told Fitzgerald about a conversation he had with Viveca Novak of *Time*. He revealed that she told him that Rove was Cooper's source, which in turn sparked him to search for e-mails about Cooper. In December 2005, both Luskin and Viveca Novak would testify about these conversations.

There is nothing that makes sense in this aspect of the story, and much that is revealing. As Isikoff and David Corn's book *Hubris* recounts, the e-mail was printed from Rove's government computer on November 25, 2003.[208] Yet this was before the FBI started focusing on Cooper.[209] It was also before Rove testified to the grand jury in February 2004, which would have allowed Rove to admit to the conversation, which he didn't do. And it was a full eleven months before Rove turned over the e-mail to Fitzgerald. Plus, there are discrepancies between Viveca Novak's story and Luskin's.[210] She says she told Luskin about Rove being Cooper's source sometime in spring 2004, no earlier than January, whereas he says it took place before the e-mail was printed off the computer, in fall 2003.

Rove and Luskin certainly did not present a plausible story to explain Rove's belated memories of his conversation with Cooper. Yet it was apparently enough to make it harder to prosecute Rove on a perjury charge.

Viveca Novak's involvement in the case is a good example of how the press was compromised, and how administration officials used the media to achieve their self-serving goals. Viveca Novak admits to having met with Luskin five times between fall 2003 and fall 2004, and she identifies the time frame for four of those meetings, all of them critical periods for Rove's involvement.[211] Yet after two of those meetings, she reported nothing on the CIA leak. In spite of their important timing, she got little worth reporting out of her meetings with Luskin.[212] He did, however. Using the taunt "Karl doesn't have a Cooper problem. He was not a source for Matt," Luskin incited her to reveal that Cooper's source was Rove.[213] Note, too, that Luskin claims this conversation took place around the same time as the *Time* magazine article (co-authored by Viveca Novak) that insisted no journalists would reveal their sources.

In the end, Rove did not get indicted for lying about his story to the FBI and the grand jury. Rove testified a fifth time on April 26, 2006. Then, after much speculation that he was about to be indicted, Fitzgerald told Luskin on June 12 that he did not anticipate bringing charges against Rove, perhaps because the witnesses against Rove were not strong enough for him to bring a case.

It is undeniable that Rove worked the press to full advantage. Rove guided the direction of journalists' coverage, casting guilt in other directions. He flipped the reporting relationship on its head, collecting key information for his defense from journalists while they sat on their own knowledge of Rove's role. Some journalists, too, seemed fearful that by telling the truth, they would lose access. But the only thing that access gets them, it seems, is the right to be spun mercilessly.

Most of all, the journalists simply lost the story line. Over the course of three years of gradually revealed involvement in the CIA leak, Karl Rove has admitted to being a central player in the leaks of Valerie Wilson's identity. He has admitted that when Robert Novak called him on July 8 or 9 of 2003 and told him he had heard that Valerie Wilson suggested Joe Wilson for the trip to Niger, Rove said, "Oh, you heard that too?"[214] On the morning of July 11, Rove passed this information on, telling Scooter Libby that Novak would be writing a story about Wilson's wife.[215] And later that same day, Rove accepted a call from Matt Cooper and talked about the

Niger allegations, telling Cooper of Valerie Wilson's CIA employ. Later, after Novak's article outed Valerie Wilson on July 14, Rove called NBC political talk show host Chris Matthews and explained that the Wilsons "were trying to screw the White House so the White House was going to screw them back" and that now that Novak had published Valerie Wilson's identity, Wilson's wife was "fair game."[216] Between his conversations with Novak, Libby, Cooper, and Matthews, then, Karl Rove had twice spread information about Valerie Wilson's employment by the CIA, discussed the publication of her identity, and pushed a journalist to pick up on the story of her identity.

And it gets worse. Take a September 2006 syndicated column from über–D.C.–insider David Broder. He doesn't tell the story of Rove's implication in a nasty leak. Instead, Broder makes two or three errors of fact, then deigns to lecture others about their reports on the CIA leak:[217] "And all of journalism needs to relearn the lesson: Can the conspiracy theories and stick to the facts."[218] Then, remarkably, he calls on some journalists to apologize to Rove! Perhaps the celebrity journalists owe an apology to the American people for failing to tell the truth about Rove's role in the CIA leak case, indictment or not.

Rove's involvement may not constitute a crime. But it violates every standard of decency, service to the nation, and commitment to national security. And yet journalists never told the story about a paid public servant cynically ruining the life work of a spy who was trying to keep the nation safe from WMDs.

CHAPTER 7

# THE FALL GUY
(September 2005–December 2006)

*[W]hat we have when someone charges obstruction of justice, the umpire gets sand thrown in his eyes. He's trying to figure what happened and somebody blocked their view.* — Patrick Fitzgerald, Press Conference, October 28, 2005

The opening scene of I. Lewis "Scooter" Libby's novel portrays an apprentice innkeeper huddled at the top of dark steps overlooking the entrance to the inn, observing new visitors. He tries to discern whether their responses to the housekeeper's questions—about whether they had been exposed to smallpox, whether they threatened the security of the inn—are true or false. The apprentice remains nameless and, like power relationships in the novel, unseen: "It occurred to [the apprentice] in the dark at the top of the staircase that none of them knew he was there."[219]

Over the course of the novel, the apprentice learns little about running an inn. But he does receive an education in unraveling enigmas. The novel, set in northern Japan at the turn of the last century, culminates in the wisdom that enigmas lurk everywhere, that everyone is hiding a secret:

"Some thought you might have something you would not want them to see."

"And they do not? Each of them? They harbor things they do not show themselves."

Such is the lifelong creative expression of Libby, the vice president's former chief of staff and national security advisor. He equates maturation with the discovery of enigma, in which behind every visible appearance there are unseen secrets.

It's a relevant theme, applicable to Libby's role in the Bush administration. Before October 28, 2005, when he was indicted and resigned his government position, few Americans had heard of Libby. That was partly by design. Libby avoided being quoted by the press. If he was seen, it was usually standing silently behind Dick Cheney. If his words were read, he was usually being quoted anonymously in news reports. Libby did serve as the source for many stories, particularly relating to weapons of mass destruction or infighting within the administration. But he usually appeared as "senior administration official."[220]

As an anonymous source, Libby largely spoke for Cheney. Their relationship dates back to the late 1980s. Libby first entered government in 1981, when his former Yale professor Paul Wolfowitz, then director of policy planning at the State Department, hired him as a staffer. When Wolfowitz moved to the Department of Defense in 1989, he brought Libby along as the deputy undersecretary of defense for strategy and resources. Cheney was then the secretary of defense for President George H. W. Bush, and thus Libby's boss.

Under Cheney's supervision, Libby oversaw the production of the first Defense Planning Guidance—a statement of the country's strategic goals— produced after the fall of the Soviet Union. The paper advocated projecting such overwhelming military power abroad that any potential rivals would not dare to compete. When the document got leaked to *The New York Times* "by an official who believes this...debate should be carried out in the public domain," the public was shocked at the naked aggression of the strategy espoused in it.[221] Arguably, the paper advocated the kind of policy we see behind the Iraq War and subsequent occupation:

> In the Middle East and Southwest Asia, our overall objective is to remain the predominant outside power in the region and preserve U.S. and Western access to the region's oil.[222]

After the uproar, the document was rewritten and softened. But with the belligerent ideas expressed in both drafts—unilateral preemption, absolute military superiority, and access to oil—Libby gave voice to an aggressive policy Cheney happily adopted as his own.[223] As the deputy undersecretary of defense for policy, Libby supported Cheney's leadership during the invasion of Panama (1989) and Operation Desert Storm (1991).

A decade later, in 2001, when Cheney brought Libby in as his chief of staff and national security advisor, Libby set up and ran Cheney's "shadow National Security Council," a set of Cheney loyalists in key positions throughout the national security establishment that would deliver on Cheney's goals, even at the expense of the administration's stated goals.[224] And if that didn't work, these loyalists—called spies by some—would report back to Libby and Cheney so as to better outflank their bureaucratic opponents.[225] As for Libby himself, his ability to serve as a caretaker for Cheney's policies was aided by his triple role: He was chief of staff and national security advisor for Cheney, but also an assistant to the president, giving him an omnipresence that often went unnoticed.

Libby was also seen as Cheney's chief propagandist when it came to selling the Iraq War. With a few other Cheney loyalists, Libby crafted some of the most inflammatory statements about Iraq's WMD, including claims of ties between Al Qaeda and Iraq and, notably, an early draft of Secretary of State Colin Powell's UN speech that had to be completely scrapped because it contained many unsubstantiated statements.[226] Often rejected by the intelligence community, Libby's efforts succeeded in pushing the limits of rhetoric about the war within the public sphere.

In short, in both his managerial and propaganda roles, Libby provided the largely unseen but highly effective infrastructure to implement Dick Cheney's aggressive policies. Cheney is widely considered the most powerful vice president in American history. And Libby has been called "Cheney's Cheney," expressing just how central he was to Cheney's ability to dominate administration policy making.

\* \* \*

For much of the period of the CIA leak investigation, no one scrutinized Libby's role closely. After all, White House strategist Karl Rove was in many ways the poster boy for smear politics, and he had already been implicated in the leak. Compared to Rove, Libby's role in the administration was unknown and little understood. But that changed in the summer and fall of 2005, when a journalist was sent to jail for not revealing her sources.

Judith Miller of *The New York Times* became one of the central figures in the drama when Special Counsel Patrick Fitzgerald issued her a subpoena because he found that Libby's notes indicated he had been directed to leak something to Miller. After refusing to comply with the subpoena, Miller was sent to jail on July 6, 2005.

On October 28, 2005, the grand jury empaneled to investigate the leak was to expire. In addition to causing concern inside the White House about possible indictments, this deadline also guaranteed a change in Miller's status. Her civil contempt imprisonment would last only as long as the grand jury term. On October 28, either she would go free or Fitzgerald would have to bring a criminal contempt charge against her, complete with a jury trial.

Of course, a third possibility existed: Miller could walk out of jail immediately if she agreed to testify. She was unwilling to do so because she believed she didn't have a personal waiver from Libby that freed her to talk about their conversations from the summer of 2003. Two things eventually changed her willingness to consider a waiver. She got her own lawyer, Robert Bennett; unlike the *Times's* lawyer, he believed Fitzgerald might bring a criminal contempt charge against her. And Fitzgerald, responding to press coverage suggesting that Miller believed she didn't have a personal waiver from Libby, pressed Libby to grant her such a waiver.[227] "Any communication reaffirming Mr. Libby's waiver…would be viewed as cooperation with the investigation," Fitzgerald wrote to Libby's lawyer.[228] The letter put the ball back in Libby's court. To maintain the appearance that he—and the Bush administration as a whole—was cooperating with the investigation, Libby had to reiterate his waiver for Miller to testify. Fitzgerald also made it easier for Miller to accept the waiver by agreeing to limit her testimony to Libby (as he had earlier limited testimony with Robert Novak and *Time's* Matthew Cooper).

Fitzgerald's strategy worked. On September 15, Libby sent Miller a letter reiterating his waiver. He followed that with a September 19 phone call to her in jail. Ten days later Miller walked out of jail so she could testify the next day.

But Libby, like others in the White House, had reason to worry about what Miller would tell the grand jury, as well as about what indictments Fitzgerald would issue before the October 28 deadline. So it was perhaps no surprise that Libby's waiver letter of September 15 wasn't just a simple waiver letter. It ended with an enigmatic appeal to solidarity:

> You went into jail in the summer. It is fall now. You will have stories to cover—Iraqi elections and suicide bombers, biological threats and the Iranian nuclear program. Out West, where you vacation, the aspens will already be turning. They turn in clusters, because their roots connect them. Come back to work—and life.[229]

Miller admitted she recognized this as a reference to an encounter she and Libby had had in 2003:

> I told the grand jury about my last encounter with Mr. Libby. It came in August 2003, shortly after I attended a conference on national security issues held in Aspen, Colo. After the conference, I traveled to Jackson Hole, Wyo. At a rodeo one afternoon, a man in jeans, a cowboy hat and sunglasses approached me. He asked me how the Aspen conference had gone. I had no idea who he was.
>
>   "Judy," he said. "It's Scooter Libby."[230]

Miller's recognition of the reference certainly suggests Libby may have been trying to send a message about cooperating. It's notable, too, that Cheney maintains a home in Jackson Hole; Libby often traveled there with the vice president. When asked if she met the vice president on that trip to Jackson Hole, Miller did not respond.[231]

Miller also recognized the risk inherent in the rest of the letter. Fitzgerald questioned her about the following passage: "As I am sure will not be news to you, the public report of every other reporter's testimony makes clear that they did not discuss Ms. Plame's name or identity with me, or knew about her before our call." Miller said she told the grand jury that the comment might be seen as an effort to coach her:

> The prosecutor asked my reaction to those words. I replied that this portion of the letter had surprised me because it might be perceived as an effort by Mr. Libby to suggest that I, too, would say we had not discussed Ms. Plame's identity.

Furthermore, press reports detailing Libby's testimony appeared in top newspapers on September 30, the morning Miller testified, which was seen by some as another effort, on the part of Libby or his surrogates, to coach Miller. A story in *The Washington Post,* for example, described Libby's version of two conversations with Miller, on July 8 and July 12. It said that at the July 8 meeting, Miller, not Libby, raised the issue of Joe Wilson. And then it parrots Libby's testimony with regard to his professed ignorance of Valerie Wilson's role on July 8 and his preliminary efforts to determine what her role was:

> Libby, the source familiar with his account said, told her that the White House was working with the CIA to find out more about Wilson's trip and how he was selected.
>
> Libby told Miller he heard that Wilson's wife had something to do with sending him but he did not know who she was or where she worked, the source said.[232]

On July 12, the article claimed, Libby finally told Miller of Valerie Wilson's involvement at the CIA—but not her name or her role as a covert operative. This version correlated with Libby's grand jury testimony that he learned of her identity from journalists, then passed it on to other journalists later in the week. It also denies that there was any mention of the two items pertinent to a violation of the Intelligence Identities Protection Act: Valerie Wilson's name and her covert status.

If Miller took the cues from Libby, she would have testified that she was the first one to raise the topic of Joe Wilson. She would have explained that in response, Libby hinted he had heard that Wilson's wife might have had a role in his trip, but that he didn't know what that was. And she would have said that only later in the week, after Libby had claimed to have learned of Valerie Wilson's identity from Tim Russert on July 10, did Libby share that information with Miller.

Apparently, truth got in the way of such testimony. Fitzgerald's subpoena to Miller—as to all other journalists—requested testimony only about conversations occurring after July 6, 2003.[233] But in her grand jury appearance on September 30, Fitzgerald asked Miller about a meeting she had had with Libby on June 23, 2003, a meeting he had learned about from the visitor logs to the office building where Libby worked.

After her first appearance before the grand jury, Miller looked for and discovered notes from that meeting. They showed that Libby raised the topic of Wilson and referred to him as a "clandestine guy." Her notes also showed that Libby brought up Valerie Wilson; in response, Miller wrote the question, "Wife works in bureau?" Miller told the grand jury that she understood the notation "bureau" to mean the CIA, given the context of her conversation with Libby.

Once Miller discovered her notes from this earlier period, there was no way her testimony could corroborate Libby's. It was clear Libby had raised Valerie Wilson's CIA employment more than two weeks before he claimed to have learned about her from Tim Russert on July 10, 2003.

On October 12, Miller went back before the grand jury and testified about the June 23 meeting—a meeting that Libby had never mentioned. Her testimony discredited Libby's story in other ways. Miller's notes showed that Libby had asked her to attribute their conversation not to a "senior administration official" but to a "former Hill staffer." The attribution was technically true—Libby had worked as the legal advisor to a House committee investigating Chinese weapons proliferation in the late 1990s—but it would clearly be misleading. It was an unusual request from Libby, suggesting that whatever he shared with Miller on July 8, he wanted to make sure it wasn't connected with the administration.

One more detail was revealed during Miller's testimony: Cheney's involvement in the leak.

The day after her first testimony, an article in the *Times* quoted an unnamed "lawyer who knows Mr. Libby's account" explaining that involvement in the response to Wilson "extended as high as Mr. Cheney."[234] It said that Cheney and Libby discussed how to handle inquiries from journalists on July 12, 2003. That might explain why, during one of her grand jury appearances, Fitzgerald asked Miller about Cheney's involvement. "Mr. Fitzgerald asked whether Mr. Cheney had known what his chief aide was doing and saying.... He asked, for example, if Mr. Libby ever indicated whether Mr. Cheney had approved of his interviews with me or was aware of them. The answer was no."

With Miller's testimony, Fitzgerald put the last piece of a puzzle in place. Miller's story about Libby's comments on June 23 and July 8 showed that two days—even two weeks—before Libby spoke to Russert, he already knew of, and was spreading news of, Valerie Wilson's identity. Miller's testimony also ruled out the possibility that Libby had learned of Wilson's identity from a journalist. Miller was clear—Libby had brought up Valerie Wilson's CIA employment, not vice versa. With this testimony, Fitzgerald could draw up an indictment.

And then the White House hunkered down in a panic, preparing for the worst as the October 28 deadline approached.

\* \* \*

Midmorning on October 28, 2005, a press advisory was posted on the newly created website for the special counsel, announcing a 2 P.M. press conference regarding the "status of the Special Counsel's criminal investigations." Between the morning announcement and the press conference itself, word slowly leaked out. Scooter Libby. Five counts. Just Scooter Libby. At 1:08 P.M., Libby offered his resignation, effective immediately.

At two o'clock, Fitzgerald stood at a lectern in a conference room at the Department of Justice, a grayish-blue curtain with a departmental logo—

the banal backdrop of bureaucracy—behind him and a roomful of journalists in front of him. Fitzgerald looked nervous; it seemed he never took a breath, and his voice shook at times. He spoke mostly without notes, though the few times he consulted his notes, the microphones picked up the crisp sound of the flapping papers. He summarized his charge simply:

> It was known that a CIA officer's identity was blown, it was known that there was a leak. We needed to figure out how that happened, who did it, why, whether a crime was committed, whether we could prove it, whether we should prove it.

He announced that the grand jury had returned an indictment of I. Lewis "Scooter" Libby, the vice president's chief of staff, on five counts: Obstruction of justice, two counts of perjury, and two counts of false statements.[235]

The obstruction charge alleged that Libby had prevented the grand jury from determining what he knew, when he knew it, and what he leaked to journalists. The remaining charges accused Libby of telling the same two lies, first to the FBI in fall 2003 and then to the grand jury in spring 2004. The first lie related to Libby's claim to have learned of Valerie Wilson's identity from Tim Russert on July 10, 2003; as Fitzgerald explained, Libby had actually learned it a month earlier from three different sources (including Cheney). The second lie related to Libby's claim to have passed on Valerie Wilson's identity to Matt Cooper and other journalists casually, telling them he had learned her identity from other journalists and didn't know whether it was true. The indictment alleged that in fact Libby had passed it on with none of these qualifications.

Basically, Fitzgerald argued that by telling these two lies, Libby had prevented the investigation from finding out whether anyone had violated the IIPA. As Fitzgerald wrote later in a court filing, Libby had told lies "to mislead and deceive both federal investigators and the grand jury as to how and when defendant acquired and disclosed to reporters information concerning the employment of Ms. Wilson by the CIA."[236]

Libby became one of the highest ranking officials to be indicted in U.S. history. Upon his resignation, both Bush and Cheney made statements of support for him. Cheney expressed regret, then said:

Scooter Libby is one of the most capable and talented individuals I have ever known. He has given many years of his life to public service and has served our nation tirelessly and with great distinction.[237]

\*    \*    \*

In one sense, the charges were anticlimactic. There was no mention of an IIPA violation, the charge Fitzgerald set out to investigate. Yet even those who, before the indictment was handed down, had clamored that Fitzgerald must avoid indicting on perjury if he didn't indict on the underlying charge quieted down when they read the indictment. It revealed the reality behind the deceptions the administration had propagated about the leak. The indictment told the story of a concerted, prolonged plan for retribution that long preceded Joe Wilson's op-ed in the *Times* on July 6, 2003.

The efforts to smear an administration critic began in response to Nicholas Kristof's column in the *Times* on May 6, 2003, reporting that an unnamed ambassador had debunked the Iraq-Niger uranium deal.[238] Libby didn't get the information about Wilson and his wife from the State Department's INR memo; in fact, that memo was drafted *in response to* Libby's request for information on Wilson. On May 29—the same day George Bush falsely proclaimed we had found WMDs in Iraq—Libby asked Marc Grossman, the undersecretary of state for political affairs, for information on the trip to Niger; Grossman told Libby that Wilson was the ambassador named in Kristof's column. Grossman gave a briefing in the White House on June 11 or 12 and passed on the erroneous information included in the INR memo: the suggestion that Valerie Wilson had convened the meeting at which Joe Wilson was given the assignment to Niger. Libby sought information from the CIA, too. On June 9, the CIA faxed a series of documents pertaining to Wilson's trip to the vice president's office, almost certainly including the report from Wilson's trip itself.[239]

By this point, Libby knew Joe Wilson's identity from Grossman, and he knew Valerie Wilson's purported role in her husband's trip from Grossman (and a CIA manager). Moreover, he had read the distorted version of Wilson's trip results portrayed in the CIA report. But Libby learned the key piece of information from Vice President Cheney himself on June 12.

According to Libby's own notes, Cheney told him that Valerie Wilson worked at the CIA in the counterproliferation division (CPD). As an expert in intelligence and security, Libby certainly knew that the CPD was on the Operations, or clandestine, side of the CIA, and that the identity of most people who worked there was classified. While Fitzgerald never claimed in the indictment that Libby knew of Wilson's covert identity, he demonstrated that Libby betrayed an awareness of the sensitive nature of her identity when he told White House press secretary Ari Fleischer that her identity was "hush hush," "it's on the QT."[240]

The collection of all this information—Wilson's identity, the results of his trip, and Valerie Wilson's employ at the CIA—predated Wilson going public with his claims. It even predated Richard Armitage telling Bob Woodward of *The Washington Post* about Valerie Wilson's identity on June 13.

Therein lies the genius of Libby's defense, much as it relies on utterly improbable stories. By claiming to have learned of Valerie Wilson's identity from Russert on July 10, Libby divorced the scheming that took place in the previous two months from the leaks of the week of July 6. By sticking to his story, Libby became the fall guy. He prevented Fitzgerald from connecting all of this deliberate, malicious data collection to the events of the week of July 6, 2003.

More important, Libby's version protected Cheney, Rove, and several others. By claiming to be the source of the leak to Matt Cooper of *Time,* Libby hid Rove's involvement. By (apparently) claiming to be the source of the leak to *The Washington Post,* Libby hid Walter Pincus's source. And as long as Libby claimed to have learned of Valerie Wilson from Russert on July 10, Fitzgerald could not tie the leaks directly to Cheney's conversations with Libby on June 12 and July 12.

Libby certainly assembled a defense team that specializes in fall guys. Along with the brilliant trial lawyer Ted Wells, Libby hired two lawyers who had defended those who took the fall in executive-branch conspiracies of the past: William Jeffress, who prevented the media from getting the White House tapes of President Richard Nixon until after all the appeals for the Watergate burglars were complete; and John Cline, who helped Oliver North limit the damage of the Iran-Contra scandal of the mid-1980s by forcing the government to either release highly classified information or dismiss charges against North. Finally, Libby's $5 million defense fund, financed by Cheney loyalists and even some people directly implicated in drumming up the case for war, served to defend the war efforts as a unit, rather than just Libby.[241]

\* \* \*

Fitzgerald scrupulously maintained the secrecy of the grand jury process, ensuring that only documents related to Libby's indictment would be revealed. But between November 2005, just after the indictment, and December 2006, Libby's lawyers and Fitzgerald carried out an ongoing battle over what evidence and what witnesses could be introduced at the trial, which was scheduled for January 2007. The many court filings submitted as part of this battle have revealed a great deal more about Cheney's close involvement in smearing Joe Wilson.

Most shocking, perhaps, is a copy of Joe Wilson's *Times* op-ed—annotated by Cheney—that was entered into evidence by Fitzgerald on May 12, 2006. On it, Cheney laid out several of the talking points used during the week of July 7, 2003:

> Have they done this sort of thing?
> Send an Amb to answer a question?
> Do we ordinarily send people out pro bono to work for us?
> Or did his wife send him on a junket?[242]

It's worth noting that the notion of Valerie Wilson sending her husband on a "junket" bears a striking similarity to the leak that Walter Pincus of the *Post* received on July 12, the day that Libby and Cheney strategized responses to the media while on board Air Force Two. Pincus's source told him that the White House had ignored Wilson's trip to Niger "because it was set up as a boondoggle by his wife, an analyst with the agency working on weapons of mass destruction."[243] Junket, boondoggle. A patently ridiculous claim about a former diplomat's trip to one of the poorest countries on earth.

When Libby was asked during a grand jury appearance on March 24, 2004, whether the "junket" claim annotated on Wilson's op-ed came up between him and Cheney during the week of July 6, Libby stammered out an unconvincing answer:

Q: And lastly it says, "Or did his wife send him on a junket?" Do you recall the Vice-President indicating or asking you or anyone in your presence whether or not Ambassador Wilson's wife had arranged to have him sent on a junket?

A: I think I recall him—I don't recall him asking me that particular question, but I think I recall him musing about that.

Q: Okay, and do you recall when it was that he mused about that?

A: I think it was after the Wilson column.

Q: Okay, and obviously—

A: I don't mean the Wilson column, I'm sorry, I misspoke. I think it was after the Novak column.

Q: Okay. And you mentioned last time that you thought [what] he had written, handwritten here, may have been discussed at a later date, like August or September by the Vice-President?

A: Yes, sir.

Q: And—

A: I don't know, later. I don't know when, but yes.

Q: Okay. And can you tell us why it would be that the Vice-President read the Novak column and had the questions, some of which apparently seem to be answered by the Novak column, would go back and pull out an original July 6th Op-Ed piece and write on that?[244]

As the exasperated questioner noted, it made no sense for Cheney to muse about Valerie Wilson's role with Libby *after* the July 14 Novak column, which asserted Cheney's central claim as a fact: "Wilson never worked for the CIA, but his wife, Valerie Plame, is an agency operative on weapons of mass destruction. Two senior administration officials told me that Wilson's wife suggested sending him to Niger. . . ." The time for musing had already passed.

* * *

One other thing dribbled out of Fitzgerald's court filings: A suggestion that Dick Cheney—and President Bush—may have been much more involved in the leak of Valerie Wilson's identity than has been known until now.

The issue revolves around the meeting that Libby had with Miller of the *Times* on July 8, 2003. As Fitzgerald revealed, Libby had instructions in his notes that when he met with Miller that day, he should leak something to her.[245] Libby told the FBI the note referred to portions of the National Intelligence Estimate on Iraq that refuted Joe Wilson, not to Valerie Wilson's identity. As Fitzgerald told the court: "Mr. Libby had an instruction to tell information to Ms. Miller on July 8 and he's saying the instruction reflected in his notes to tell…Judith Miller refers to the NIE. He says he did not discuss Mr. Wilson's wife that day. To our understand[ing] both were discussed."[246]

Libby's lawyer, Ted Wells, downplays the significance of this note, arguing that this NIE leaking was part of a larger campaign designed to prove three things: that Joe Wilson had not seen and debunked the forgeries alleging a Niger uranium deal, that Wilson had not been sent to Niger by Cheney, and that the NIE supported the claims about Iraq's attempts to acquire uranium. Wells is correct that leaking the NIE was part of a larger campaign. Bob Woodward has said that Libby leaked him the NIE on June 27.[247] Libby also leaked portions of it to the *Times*'s David Sanger on July 2.[248] And Miller admits that Libby shared details of the NIE. Finally, we have the *Wall Street Journal* article that we now know arose because Libby instructed someone to leak the NIE to the *Journal*.[249] So it's clear that, as Libby has testified, he leaked portions of the NIE to at least four journalists, in June and July.

But the explanation doesn't hold up—not when we learn how unusual Libby's meeting with Miller was on July 8. Libby treated it quite differently than he did the others. For example, Libby met Miller in person to leak this information, rather than having another person pass on the information as he did with the *Journal*. To leak the NIE, Libby met Woodward in his office. But when it came to Miller, he met her at the ritzy St. Regis Hotel, two blocks north of the White House. Libby testified that "one of the reasons why he met with Miller at a hotel was the fact that he was sharing this information with Miller exclusively."[250] And at this meeting, Libby took the unusual step of asking Miller to refer to him as a "former Hill staffer" rather than as a "senior administration official."

But the *real* difference in Libby's treatment of Miller lies in the approval he obtained for it. In his testimony, Libby admitted that he didn't know whether he was authorized to leak the NIE materials when he leaked them to Sanger (and possibly Woodward); he said he may have received authorization, relied on public statements made by National Security Advisor Condoleezza Rice, or just "slipped."[251]

But leaking to Miller somehow required approval from a higher authority. When Cheney directed him to leak material to Miller, Libby objected that he couldn't share it with Miller because it was classified. Cheney assured Libby he would get authorization from the president, which he then did, telling Libby that Bush had personally authorized the leak. For Libby, that still wasn't enough. Sometime after July 6, Libby asked David Addington, then counsel to the vice president, whether the president could unilaterally declassify information. Addington assured him the president had that authority. Libby testified that this July 8 conversation with Miller was "the only time he recalled in his government experience when he disclosed a document to a reporter that was effectively declassified by virtue of the President's authorization that it be disclosed."[252] Libby had worked in and out of government for almost twenty-five years, so this was clearly a unique event.

The notion that leaking the NIE to Miller was a unique event is a tough sell, because Miller already had been leaked two of the other key claims in the NIE relating to Saddam's intent to acquire nuclear weapons. For example, a text box in the NIE reported the claims of a defector, Adnan Ihsan Saeed al-Haideri, which was information Miller had learned back in December 2001, when she interviewed Haideri personally. Miller (with her colleague Michael Gordon) had also been leaked the discussion about the aluminum tubes back in September 2002. Miller fairly routinely received classified leaks regarding WMDs.[253]

All of which suggests the question: Is it possible that Cheney didn't direct Libby to share the NIE with Judith Miller on July 8, but directed him to leak something else to her—a much more unusual kind of leak?

Fitzgerald doesn't specify what Miller received that Woodward and Sanger didn't—he says only they received "substantially less information" than Miller.[254] He does make clear though that Libby leaked more than just the NIE to Miller that day: "In that meeting with Ms. Miller, defendant discussed, among other things, Mr. Wilson's Op-Ed, Mr. Wilson's trip to Niger, portions of the October 2002 NIE—and the CIA employment of Ms. Wilson."[255]

That is, the substantially different information that got leaked to Miller, compared to the other journalists, pertains to Wilson's trip report and Valerie Wilson's CIA employment.

The possibility is not something Cheney will deny—at least not publicly. On a September 10, 2006, appearance on NBC's *Meet the Press*, Cheney was asked about what he directed Libby to leak:

RUSSERT: Let me turn back home, domestic politics, and talk about the whole situation involving Scooter Libby, your former chief of staff, who was indicted by Patrick Fitzgerald. This was a document that was released in the investigation. It's a *New York Times* op-ed piece with your handwriting on it. And that handwriting says, "Or did his wife send him on a junket?" referring to Ambassador Joe Wilson's wife, Valerie Plame, who was a CIA, CIA agent. Did you, in any way, authorize Scooter Libby to release her name or her occupation to the press?

CHENEY: Tim, Scooter Libby is, he's a good man. He's a friend of mine. He's somebody—one of the most competent and capable people I've ever known. He's entitled to the presumption of innocence. But there is a legal matter pending, there is going to be a trial next year, I could well be a witness in the trial, and much as I would like to talk about, and I certainly have strong opinions about the case, I think it'd be totally inappropriate for me to do so.

RUSSERT: There was a story in the *National Journal* that Cheney authorized Libby to leak confidential information. Can you confirm or deny that?

CHENEY: I have the authority as vice president under executive order issued by the president to classify and declassify information. And everything I've done is consistent with those authorities.

RUSSERT: Could you declassify Valerie Plame's status as an operative?

CHENEY: I've said all I'm going to say on the subject, Tim.[256]

Libby was charged with obstructing an investigation into the activities of a number of people, including the vice president. After his trial in 2007, Libby will either be found guilty or he will walk. Yet that verdict will not end the story. The activities of others may remain beyond the reach of Fitzgerald's investigation, because of Libby's alleged obstruction as well as constitutional limits. Cheney may continue to refuse to answer questions, and the media may stop asking the important questions. But that doesn't mean the citizens of the United States should let it rest. If the deceptions that brought us into the Iraq War have taught us anything, it is that we, as citizens, must ask the questions to reveal the truth. And there are still a lot of questions left unanswered.

# EPILOGUE
December 2006

It's kind of awkward, telling a story before you know how it ends. I'm finishing this book about six weeks before the scheduled start date of Scooter Libby's trial, so I don't know how it will turn out. But to a large degree, that doesn't matter. From the look of things in Washington, D.C., this book will remain pertinent long after the legal proceedings are over.

For all its unique scope and striking characters, the CIA leak case is in many ways just the archetypal story of the failures of insider D.C. culture, in which reporters have become so addicted to access that they can no longer report responsibly on the workings of our nation's capital.

Perhaps the most damning expression of the problem, with respect to the CIA leak case, comes from *The Washington Post*'s syndicated columnist Richard Cohen in an October 13, 2005, column titled "Let This Leak Go." Cohen pleads with special prosecutor Patrick Fitzgerald to just move on ("Go home, Pat") rather than indict anyone on the charge of perjury. He goes on to claim this case will have a chilling effect on the press's ability to monitor the government because it will discourage leaks…but it seems that Cohen's biggest concern about leaks is that he hasn't gotten any; Fitzgerald has maintained the "creepy silence" legally required of grand jury proceedings. Cohen is basically making the case that the press should retain exclusive judgment on the behavior of politicians, with no role for the courts. But then he proves just why he cannot be trusted with such judgment: He dismisses the leak and its consequences as banal D.C. fare.

> Not nice, but it was what Washington does day in and day out.... This is rarely considered a crime. In the Plame case, it might technically be one, but it was not the intent of anyone to out a CIA agent and have her assassinated (which happened once) but to assassinate the character of her husband. This is an entirely different thing. She got hit by a ricochet.

In D.C. this may be easy to dismiss—Valerie Plame Wilson's entire life's work protecting our country from WMDs as mere collateral damage in a nasty game of pinball. The character assassination of someone who tried to serve his country—that, too, is just part of the game to Cohen. But to me, watching this from the provincial perspective of Michigan, even suggesting such a thing is a betrayal of our nation's welfare. Cohen reflects the culture that breeds this indifference when he describes the journalists' motivations as "pursuit of truth, fame and choice restaurant tables." Restaurant tables.

The D.C. journalists—many of them, anyway—seem to see everything as this kind of game. Whether the administration is lying about the cost of Medicare, the beneficiaries of its tax cuts, or the intelligence behind its case for war, the D.C. press corps seem to have lost any understanding that the events they narrate have consequences. They're more interested in who wins the spin game than whether the American people win or lose. And as a result, they treat getting spun, badly, as just one more play in a game in which the stakes are no higher than a fistful of cocktail weenies.

From that perspective, then, this book is more than a story about Valerie Plame Wilson, the men who ruined her career, and the unflappable prosecutor who tried to bring those men to justice. It's a story about an ongoing threat to our democracy. It's a story about what happens when those we employ to expose the workings and abuses of power instead get giddily seduced by that power. At this point, it seems, the welfare of our country is being bargained away for a window table in some posh D.C. restaurant.

It may be too much to hope that with yet another reminder, the Beltway insiders might finally realize that, as Jon Stewart once said, they're "hurting America." Barring that outcome, I hope this book, in exposing the anatomy of this deceit, might serve as encouragement. It doesn't take the backing of newspapers with declining circulation and crowds of insider sources to contribute to holding our government accountable. It takes time, persistence, and an effort to read through the spin. It's something every citizen can do. And it's something we need to do to keep our government honest.

# TIMELINE

## 1992–2002: LAYING THE GROUNDWORK FOR WAR

### 1992

I. Lewis "Scooter" Libby guides the production of the first Defense Planning Guidance document drafted after the end of the Cold War. It calls for preventing any country from growing strong enough to rival the United States. It is considered the first expression of neoconservative policy and is one reason behind Dick Cheney's respect for Scooter Libby.

### August 1995

Saddam Hussein's brother-in-law Hussein Kamel defects to Jordan and reveals full extent of Iraqi weapons of mass destruction (WMD) programs, but tells U.S. and international weapons inspectors that Iraq destroyed them all.

### January 24, 1998

Weapons inspector Scott Ritter briefs Iraqi defector Ahmed Chalabi on UN weapons inspectors' expectations in Iraq. Ritter provided Chalabi a detailed description of inspectors' suspicions about mobile bioweapons labs (MBLs).

**January 26, 1998**
Members of the Project for the New American Century (PNAC), a group closely tied to the hawkish neoconservative movement, send President Bill Clinton a letter urging him to support a policy for regime change in Iraq. Signatories to the letter include:

- Elliott Abrams, who would become George W. Bush's top Middle East advisor and later his deputy national security advisor

- Richard Armitage, who would serve as deputy secretary of state under Colin Powell

- John Bolton, future undersecretary of state and UN ambassador

- Pentagon advisor Richard Perle

- Donald Rumsfeld, who would become Bush's secretary of defense

- Paul Wolfowitz, deputy secretary of defense under Rumsfeld and later president of the World Bank

- Pentagon advisor James Woolsey

Almost all of these PNAC members pushed the Bush administration to adopt a hawkish policy on Iraq.

**August 15, 1998**
Judith Miller, with James Risen, publishes a story in *The New York Times* on Khidir Hamza, an expatriate Iraqi nuclear scientist connected to Chalabi's Iraqi National Congress. Hamza claimed Iraq could develop a bomb a year or two after inspectors withdrew and sanctions ended. He is later discredited as a fraud.

**October 31, 1998**
The Iraq Liberation Act is signed into law. The law sets aside $97 million to support opposition groups in hopes of effecting a Democratic transition in Iraq. It makes "regime change" the official policy of the U.S. and starts the policy of funding the defectors who would provide dodgy intelligence to justify the war.

**December 1998**
UN weapons inspectors (UNSCOM) withdraw from Iraq to prepare for U.S. bombing campaign on Iraq. After the withdrawal of inspectors, the U.S. loses much of its ability to collect intelligence on Iraq.

**1999**
Joe Wilson conducts trip for the CIA to learn whether Pakistani nuclear scientist A. Q. Khan attempted to acquire uranium from Niger.

**February 1999**
Iraq's ambassador to the Vatican, Wissam al-Zahawie, visits Niger to invite the Nigerien president to visit Iraq. It would later be alleged that this visit pertained to arranging a uranium deal.

**Spring 1999**
Retired ambassador Joe Wilson coaches members of Niger's military government to help their transition to civilian rule.

**November 1999**
Iraqi defector "Curveball" arrives in Germany, telling stories about his personal involvement with MBLs.

**February 2000**
Antonio Nucera of SISMI, the Italian intelligence agency, introduces con man Martino Rocco to SISMI source La Signora. The meeting would lead to the production and circulation of forgeries alleging an Iraq-Niger uranium deal.

**March 2000**
A Defense Intelligence Agency medical technician first raises concerns about Curveball, believing him to be an alcoholic.

**January 2, 2001**
A break-in is reported at the Nigerien Embassy in Rome. The thieves may have provided cover for the SISMI agents producing the Niger forgeries; they may also have collected materials in the production of those forgeries.

**January 30, 2001**
At his first National Security Council meeting, President George W. Bush makes regime change in Iraq a top security policy. Defense Secretary Donald Rumsfeld promises to examine military options; CIA Director George Tenet commits to improving intelligence on Iraq.

**February 24, 2001**
Secretary of State Colin Powell asserts that the sanctions regime against Saddam has worked—he has not developed any significant WMD capabilities.

**March 2001**
The Information Collection Program, a propaganda and intelligence program, authorizes the Iraqi National Congress to to provide information to the U.S. about Saddam Hussein's regime. Under this program, the INC connected defectors—some of them fabricators— with U.S. intelligence agencies.

**April 10, 2001**
The first CIA analysis on Iraq's aluminum tubes determines they are intended for uranium enrichment.

**May 2001**
The Department of Energy (DOE) explains that the aluminum tubes almost exactly match known Iraqi rocket casings.

**June 2001**
CIA operatives—including Valerie Plame Wilson—work with Jordan to
intercept a shipment of aluminum tubes.

**July 2001**
The International Atomic Energy Agency (IAEA) agrees with DOE's judgment
that the aluminum tubes are intended for a conventional rocket program.

**September 20, 2001**
President Bush first raises the prospect of war on Iraq with British Prime
Minister Tony Blair.

**October 2001**
Creation of the Counter-Terrorism Evaluation Group, a parallel intelligence
organization developing the argument supporting the hawks' case for war,
under Cheney ally David Wurmser. The group evolves into the Office of
Special Plans.

**October 15, 2001**
The first SISMI report on Nigerien uranium is sent to CIA.

**December 20, 2001**
Judith Miller publishes a story on INC defector Adnan Haideri, who claims
Iraq had renewed its interest in nuclear weapons.

**January 29, 2002**
President Bush names Iraq as part of the "Axis of Evil."

**February 2002**
Senator Bob Graham learns that military resources are being pulled out
of Afghanistan to prepare for war against Iraq.

**February 5, 2002**
SISMI shares a second report on Nigerien uranium. This report would
spark Vice President Cheney to ask for more information on the Nigerien
uranium allegations, which would lead to Joe Wilson's Niger trip.

**February 19, 2002**
A meeting is held at CIA headquarters in Langley, Virginia, to determine whether Joe Wilson can help determine the accuracy of the Nigerien uranium claim. Valerie Wilson introduces her husband. Bureau of Intelligence and Research (INR) analyst Douglas Rohn takes notes—inaccurate notes—that will form the INR memo.

**March 25, 2002**
Third SISMI report on Nigerien uranium.

**March 2002**
Dick Cheney tells Republican senators that the U.S. will go to war against Iraq.

**June 2002**
Cheney and his national security advisor, Scooter Libby, make unprecedented trips to CIA to pressure analysts.

**June 1, 2002**
Bush announces a new policy of preemptive war.

**July 23, 2002**
The "Downing Street memo" is written by British foreign secretary Jack Straw. It states that "the intelligence and facts were being fixed around the policy" and forecasts that the campaign to build support for war to begin a month before congressional elections.

**August 2002**
The Office of Special Plans is founded, to cull raw intelligence reports and develop talking points to support the war.

White House chief of staff Andrew Card founds the White House Iraq Group to build support for war. Its members include Karl Rove, Karen Hughes, Mary Matalin, Scooter Libby, and Condoleezza Rice. WHIG's July 2003 papers would be subpoenaed in the CIA leak investigation.

**August 26, 2002**
Cheney gives a speech that has not been vetted by the CIA, nor approved by Bush. In it, he declares, "There is no doubt that Saddam Hussein has weapons of mass destruction." The speech forces the administration to adopt a confrontational stance even sooner than the White House had planned on doing.

**September 2002**
CIA's head of operations for Europe, Tyler Drumheller, learns the Germans believe Curveball may be a fabricator and may have psychological problems.

**September 5, 2002**
Senator Bob Graham of Florida, head of the Senate Intelligence Committee, learns the Bush administration has not planned to produce a National Intelligence Estimate on Iraq. Graham requests one.

**September 8, 2002**
*New York Times* reporters Michael Gordon and Judith Miller write an article describing Iraqi attempts to acquire aluminum tubes, supposedly for a uranium enrichment program. On the same day, Condoleezza Rice, Colin Powell, Dick Cheney, and Donald Rumsfeld appear on Sunday morning talk shows to make the case for war. Rice, Rumsfeld, and the *New York Times* article all use the phrase "mushroom cloud" to describe the threat of an Iraqi nuclear program.

**September 12, 2002**
Bush's speech to the UN calls for a resolution against Iraq and weapons inspectors.

**September 24, 2002**
A British white paper on the threat from Iraq is released. This was the first public mention of the Nigerien uranium allegation. The dossier would later be described as "sexed up."

**October 1, 2002**
The National Intelligence Estimate on Iraq, the intelligence community's best summary of what it knows about Iraq, is published. Cheney gives Bush a one-page summary, including details of the debate about the aluminum tubes.

**October 4–6, 2002**
CIA sends the National Security Council repeated warnings against Niger uranium claims.

**October 7, 2002**
CIA refuses to allow President Bush to use Niger claims in a speech in Cincinnati.

**October 9, 2002**
Italian journalist Elisabetta Burba receives forged documents alleging an Iraq-Niger uranium deal. She vets them with the U.S. Embassy, from which they are eventually forwarded to Cheney ally John Bolton at Department of State.

**October 11, 2002**
The Iraq War resolution is approved by the U.S. Congress.

**October 15, 2002**
A State Department INR analyst debunks the uranium documents.

**November 27, 2002**
Weapons inspectors return to Iraq.

**December 2002**
CIA's Berlin station chief warns George Tenet that Curveball may be unreliable.

**December 19, 2002**
A fact sheet drafted in John Bolton's department repeats the Niger allegation. This is the first public mention of an alleged sale of Nigerien uranium to Iraq.

# 2003: THE WAR AND THE LEAK

**January 2003**
The top intelligence officer for Africa warns the Bush administration that the Nigerien uranium claim is without merit.

**January 9, 2003**
Mohamed El Baradei, head of the IAEA, reports to the UN that the Iraqi aluminum tubes are intended for conventional rockets.

**January 28, 2003**
Bush gives his State of the Union speech, in which he utters the famous sixteen words.

**February 4, 2003**
When asked to provide additional reasons (beyond the Italian forgeries) to the IAEA for concern about the Niger allegations, the U.S. mentions the CIA report from Joe Wilson's trip. This was the first time any intelligence agency used the report to support the allegations that Iraq was attempting to acquire uranium.

**February 5, 2003**
Secretary of State Colin Powell addresses the UN, making the case for war. Powell does not mention the Niger allegation, though he does use the aluminum tubes and MBLs to defend the war.

**February 9, 2003**
The United Nations Monitoring, Verification and Inspection Commission (UNMOVIC) searches Curveball's former worksite and determines his claims about MBLs to be false.

**March 7, 2003**
IAEA announces that the documents on which the Nigerien uranium claim is based are crude forgeries. They informed the administration of this four days earlier, on March 3.

**March 8, 2003**
On CNN, Joe Wilson suggests the administration knew the Niger claims were wrong. On the same day, the DIA again uses the report on Wilson's trip to support allegations that Iraq sought uranium.

**March 16, 2003**
Dick Cheney claims, "We believe [Saddam] has, in fact, reconstituted nuclear weapons."

**March 19, 2003**
Iraq War begins.

**March 25, 2003**
Bush issues an executive order giving the vice president the power to declassify information. This act provides the legal justification for later claims that Cheney authorized the leak of the National Intelligence Estimate.

**April 5, 2003**
Judith Miller reveals a source's name, even though the source had not spoken for attribution.

**April 21, 2003**
First "Yankee Fan" article in the *Times* provides explanation for the absence of WMDs: The weapons had been destroyed.

**April 24, 2003**
Second "Yankee Fan" article.

**May 1, 2003**
Bush declares "the United States...has prevailed" in front of banner declaring MISSION ACCOMPLISHED.

Judith Miller preempts a colleague's profile of Ahmed Chalabi by publishing her own. In the profile, she quotes an anonymous source insinuating that one Chalabi ally was a CIA asset.

*New York Times* reporter Jayson Blair resigns after it is discovered he fabricated or plagiarized many of his stories. The ensuing scrutiny leads to the resignation of editors who had encouraged Miller's prewar reporting and brings her own reporting under scrutiny.

**May 6, 2003**
Nicholas Kristof publishes a column in the *Times* describing Joe Wilson's allegations. In response, Cheney's office begins to collect information on Wilson.

**May 7, 2003**
Judith Miller publishes her first Mukhabarat article, "finding" a uranium document.

**May 8, 2003**
Miller publishes first of four mobile bioweapons lab articles, admitting some doubts.

**May 9, 2003**
Miller publishes a second Mukhabarat article, reporting that most of what was found earlier has disappeared.

**May 11, 2003**
Miller publishes a second MBL article.

**May 15, 2003**
A *Times* spokesperson announces the paper will look at reporters besides Blair whose work is questionable.

**May 16, 2003**
CIA publishes a white paper on MBL. The paper dismisses Iraq's hydrogen balloons explanation as "denial and deception" and doesn't admit several discrepancies with the trailers.

**May 19, 2003**
The MBL white paper is briefed to the White House.

**May 21, 2003**
Judith Miller publishes a third MBL article (with William Broad), asserting that the trailers are definitely MBLs. The article relies on the still-classified white paper and preempts the investigation of the Jefferson Project, an international team of weapons inspectors.

**May 27, 2003**
The Jefferson Project determines the trailers are not MBLs, and so informs CIA in an e-mailed executive summary.

**May 28, 2003**
CIA's MBL white paper is declassified.

**May 29, 2003**
Bush claims that Coalition forces have found WMD, based on the MBL claims.

Cheney's office seeks information on Joe Wilson from the State Department.

**June 8, 2003**
National Security Advisor Condoleezza Rice claims no one at her level knew the Niger intelligence to be bad. Joe Wilson tries to contact her via an intermediary to correct this claim, but to no avail. This incident prompts Wilson to write his July 6 op-ed.

**June 10, 2003**
The first "INR memo" details the State Department's stance on the Niger allegations. It mentions Valerie Wilson's CIA affiliation.

**June 12, 2003**
*Washington Post* reporter Walter Pincus publishes an article describing Joe Wilson's allegations. On the same day, Cheney tells Libby that Valerie Wilson works in the counterproliferation department at CIA.

**June 13, 2003**
Deputy Secretary of State Richard Armitage tells *Washington Post* reporter Bob Woodward of Valerie Wilson's involvement in WMD at CIA.

**June 17, 2003**
CIA concludes the Niger claims are incorrect. Cheney is briefed that the CIA has withdrawn its uranium claim.

**June 19, 2003**
*The New Republic* publishes an article detailing prewar intelligence problems. It is the third article mentioning Joe Wilson discussed in Cheney's office.

**June 23, 2003**
Scooter Libby and Judith Miller meet in Libby's office. Libby suggests that Valerie Wilson may work at the CIA.

**June 27, 2003**
Libby and Bob Woodward meet in Libby's office; Libby leaks details of the NIE.

**July 6, 2003**
Joe Wilson publishes his op-ed in *The New York Times,* concluding that the Bush administration purposefully manipulated intelligence in order to win support for the war.

**July 7, 2003**
Scooter Libby tells White House spokesperson Ari Fleischer that Valerie Wilson works at the CIA.

The second "INR memo," this time addressed to Undersecretary of State Marc Grossman, Armitage, Powell, and State Department spokesperson Richard Boucher. Armitage would have it faxed to Colin Powell.

**July 8, 2003**

Meeting between Scooter Libby and Judith Miller at St. Regis Hotel. Libby leaked the NIE, the report from Wilson's trip, and (according to Miller) Valerie Wilson's role at the CIA. Libby also insinuated that Joe Wilson had an earlier liaison role between Iraq and Niger.

Possible conversation between presidential advisor Karl Rove and conservative Robert Novak about Valerie Wilson.

Robert Novak tells a complete stranger that Valerie Wilson works at the CIA on WMD.

Robert Novak and Richard Armitage meet in Armitage's office. Armitage tells Novak that Valerie Wilson works at the CIA on WMD.

**July 9, 2003**

Possible Karl Rove and Robert Novak conversation.

**July 10, 2003**

Joe Wilson calls Novak about the leak of Valerie Wilson's identity; Novak asks Wilson to confirm the report.

Libby complains to Tim Russert of NBC News about Chris Matthews's coverage of the Niger allegations. Libby later claims that Russert leaked Valerie Wilson's identity during this conversation.

**July 10 or 11, 2003**

Libby and Rove discuss Rove's conversation with Novak. Rove informs Libby that Novak will publish a story on Joe Wilson's wife.

**July 11, 2003**

Rove speaks with *Time* magazine reporter Matthew Cooper. He reveals that Valerie Wilson works at the CIA on WMD.

George Tenet accepts partial responsibility for Niger allegation being in the State of the Union speech.

**July 12, 2003**
Libby and Dick Cheney fly to Virginia on Air Force 2. They strategize on
how to respond to Wilson.

Libby talks with Cooper and confirms Valerie Wilson's employment
at the CIA.

Two Libby conversations with Miller.

Libby talks with *Washington Post* reporter Glenn Kessler. According to
Kessler, they didn't discuss Valerie Wilson.

Senior administration official informs Walter Pincus that Valerie Wilson
works at the CIA on WMD.

**July 14, 2003**
Novak column reveals that Valerie Wilson is a "operative" on WMD
and claims she sent her husband to Niger to examine allegations of
an Iraq-Niger uranium deal.

**July 16, 2003**
Journalist David Corn asks whether Novak's column amounts to a violation
of the Intelligence Identities Protection Act (IIPA).

**July 18, 2003**
The NIE on Iraq is declassified. The White House's director of communications, Dan Bartlett, gives more details in a background briefing.

**July 20, 2003**
NBC reporter Andrea Mitchell tells Wilson that the White House has
informed her that Valerie Wilson is the story, not Wilson's own allegations
that the administration manipulated intelligence to make a case for war.

**July 21, 2003**
MSNBC reporter Chris Matthews tells Joe Wilson that Karl Rove told him
Valerie Wilson was "fair game."

**July 22, 2003**
Deputy National Security Advisor Stephen Hadley and Director of Communications Dan Bartlett admit being warned by the CIA about the Niger claims in October 2002.

An article in *Newsday* by Tim Phelps and Knut Royce confirms Valerie Wilson's covert identity and quotes Novak as claiming his sources "came to him and gave him the name."

**Late July 2003**
A CIA officer explains to Scooter Libby the danger of revealing Valerie Wilson's identity.

# 2003–2006: THE INVESTIGATION

**September 26, 2003**
The Department of Justice announces an investigation into CIA leak.

**September 28, 2003**
A *Washington Post* article (known as the 1x2x6 article) strongly suggests that the leak of Valerie Wilson's identity was intentional.

**September 29, 2003**
Robert Novak and Karl Rove have a conversation about the investigation.

**October 1, 2003**
Novak publishes his "partisan gunslinger" column (the October 6 version uses the name "Flame" instead of "Plame"), backing off from his story of receiving an intentional leak.

**October 2, 2003**
FBI interviews Richard Armitage.

**October 4, 2003**
Novak reveals that Valerie Wilson used her CIA cover company,
Brewster & Jennings, on FEC records.

**October 7, 2003**
FBI interviews Novak.

Bush publicly doubts that the leaker will be found.

**October 12, 2003**
*The Washington Post*'s Mike Allen reiterates 1x2x6; the article (written
with Walter Pincus) reveals that the *Post* also received the leak.

**October 14, 2003**
FBI first interviews Libby.

**December 30, 2003**
U.S. Attorney General John Ashcroft recuses himself. Deputy Attorney
General James Comey appoints Patrick Fitzgerald as special counsel to
investigate the CIA leak.

**January 14, 2004**
Novak is interviewed at his lawyer's office.

**February 2004**
Karl Rove testifies twice before the grand jury.

**March 5, 2004**
Libby testifies before the grand jury.

**March 24, 2004**
Libby testifies again before the grand jury.

**June 2, 2004**
George W. Bush seeks private counsel.

**June 5, 2004**
*The Washington Post* confirms Fitzgerald has already interviewed Cheney.

**June 24, 2004**
Fitzgerald interviews Bush.

**August 23, 2004**
Cooper testifies, revealing that Libby was not his first source for the information that Valerie Wilson worked at the CIA. According to Cooper, Fitzgerald was surprised by the information.

**September 13, 2004**
Fitzgerald issues a more general subpoena to Matt Cooper. This is the sole subpoena in the case requiring a journalist to reveal details about an unnamed source.

**October 7, 2004**
Cooper's attempt to quash the subpoena is denied. Rove only turns over the e-mail indicating he might be Cooper's source after Cooper's subpoena is quashed, when he testifies on October 15.

**October 15, 2004**
Rove testifies a third time. He admits he may have spoken with Cooper.

**July 6, 2005**
Cooper works out a last-minute agreement to testify after Rove's lawyer claims Cooper is not protecting Rove.

Miller sent to jail for contempt of court.

**July 13, 2005**
Cooper testifies and reveals that his source was Karl Rove.

**July 14, 2005**
Democrats call on Bush to fulfill his promise to fire anyone involved in the CIA leak.

**July 15, 2005**
Stories casting suspicion on Ari Fleischer first appear. The stories would retain credence right up until the week of Libby's indictment.

**September 15, 2005**
Libby writes the "Aspen" letter to Miller, encouraging her to testify.

**September 29, 2005**
Miller agrees to testify and is released from jail.

**September 30, 2005**
Miller testifies.

**October 12, 2005**
Miller testifies a second time, about her June 23 meeting with Libby.

**October 14, 2005**
Rove testifies a fourth time.

**October 28, 2005**
Libby is indicted on five charges: two of false statements, one of obstruction, and two of perjury.

**November 14, 2005**
Bob Woodward gives a deposition about an early leak from Richard Armitage.

**December 8, 2005**
*Time* magazine reporter Viveca Novak gives a deposition about contacts with Robert Luskin, lawyer for Karl Rove.

**February 2006**
Armitage is informed he will not be charged.

**April 26, 2006**
Rove testifies for a fifth time before the grand jury.

**June 13, 2006**
Rove is informed he will not be charged.

**July 2006**
Joe and Valerie Wilson file civil suit against Cheney, Libby, Rove, and ten "John Does." They will later add Armitage.

**January 16, 2007**
Scheduled start of jury selection for Libby trial.

# ACKNOWLEDGMENTS

It's really inaccurate to have just my name on the cover of this book. It actually is the end product of a giant, ongoing conversation among hundreds of people. I only hope my effort does their contributions justice.

This book wouldn't have happened if it weren't for Jane Hamsher. The book arose out of a panel she put together at the YearlyKos convention in June 2006. Since then, she has shepherded the project to completion with real determination. I'm particularly grateful for her generosity and integrity, with me and with others, which really set her apart in the blogosphere.

Then there are the people who helped turn an endless series of blog posts into a somewhat coherent book. Safir Ahmed wisely and patiently coaxed me away from details only Plame nuts care about; he deserves credit for places where the narrative flows, while my stubborn self should get all the blame for passages that bog down in details. Will Rockafellow joined the team with little notice and managed to pull the project together.

There are many people in the blogosphere on whose work I drew heavily. On the administration's WMD claims, there's eRiposte, who awes me with his tenacious investigations of the Niger claims. FMJ, De Gondi, lukery, and Simon also provided valuable feedback on the WMD claims.

And the Plameologists — Plame bloggers and commenters — have helped me improve my understanding of this case with their own contributions and their challenges to mine. Jane Hamsher offered the best storytelling on Plame out there. Christy Hardin Smith and Jeralyn Merritt offered hours and hours of free legal expertise. Swopa really led the pack with his coverage of Plame going back to 2003. And Tom Maguire has been a good-natured adversary. I'm particularly grateful for those who commented regularly at The Next Hurrah and elsewhere—those conversations are truly at the root of this book. A few deserve special thanks: In addition to Quicksilver's poetic eye for details, he provided me with a collection of first editions of neoconservative texts that have been useful in finishing the book. Pollyusa, a kind of dedicated Plame librarian, deserves special thanks for her ability to ferret out the most obscure references immediately. And most of all, my work has been shaped by endless conversations with Jeff, both on blogs and via e-mail.

My blogmates at The Next Hurrah—DHinMI (who kindly invited me to join the blog), Kagro X, DemFromCT, Mimikatz, Plutonium Page, Sara, JamesB3, emptypockets, and Trapper John—have provided great camaraderie, and tolerance for the Plame nut in their midst. And above all, Meteor Blades offered the spark and encouragement to make this happen.

Thanks to Charles for his hospitality in San Francisco as we scrambled to pull this together.

Gail, a good friend and great boss, was incredibly flexible during the key months of this project, which allowed me the time to finish it.

And to my sweetie, Derek, you'll have your wife back soon, I promise.

*Special Thanks:* Many of the readers of Firedoglake, The Next Hurrah, DailyKos, and other blogs donated to this project. It is truly humbling to know that so many people trusted me to do justice to this project. Thank you for providing the trust, the contributions, and the community that made this book possible.

*A Note from the Publisher:* We at Vaster would also like to extend a big thank you to all those who helped make this project happen. All donations have gone to publishing and promoting Marcy's book. Any profits generated from its sale will go toward publishing more books by progressive authors.

# NOTES

**CHAPTER 1** SIXTEEN WORDS

**1.** Tom Hamburger and Peter Wallsten describe Libby and Cheney visiting the CIA twelve times, "most often to discuss Iraq's possible links to nuclear weapons and terrorism." "CIA, Cheney Long at Odds," *Los Angeles Times*, October 20, 2005.

**2.** For example, Cheney had the full ninety-page national intelligence estimate (a comprehensive report of the intelligence community on a given issue) on Iraq's WMDs but gave Bush only a one-page summary, so as to preserve the president's plausible deniability about many of the dissents in the larger document. Ron Suskind, *The One Percent Doctrine* (New York: Simon & Schuster, 2006), 174-75.

**3.** Daniel Eisenberg, "We're Taking Him Out," *Time*, May 5, 2002.

**4.** Four Democratic senators—Bob Graham, Dick Durbin, Carl Levin, and Dianne Feinstein—and one Republican—Richard Lugar—requested the production of the NIE in the second two weeks of September. Director of Central Intelligence George Tenet and the administration resisted producing the NIE, normally an important part of any major decision-making process. In the end, it was produced in three weeks, a time period so brief that many of the analysts involved complained that it affected the accuracy of the document. For example, one analyst explained, "people were coming to the table in the process that normally takes four to six months to work its way through, with several meetings and a little bit of blood on the floor, and lots of good scientific debate did not occur." Senate Select Committee on Intelligence, Report on the US Intelligence Community's Prewar Intelligence Assessments on Iraq (hereafter "SSCI"), July 7, 2004, 300.

**5.** Former Senator Bob Graham provides descriptions of the politicization surrounding the NIE in "What I Knew Before the Invasion," *The Washington Post*, November 20, 2005, and interview, "The Dark Side," *Frontline*, transcript at http://www.pbs.org/wgbh/pages/frontline/darkside/interviews/graham.html. According to Dana Priest, the unclassified NIE actually dated to May 2002. "Report Says CIA Distorted Iraq Data," *The Washington Post*, July 12, 2004.

**6.** Video link to the State of the Union speech on January 28, 2003, is at http://www.whitehouse.gov/news/releases/2003/01/20030128-19.html.

**7.** One of the word games used in the State of the Union speech was to attribute its claims to someone else, someone outside the White House. The administration would offer contradictory reasons for presenting its sources so forwardly. According to a July 22 press conference by White House Communications Director Dan Bartlett and Deputy National Security Advisor Stephen Hadley, a group of administration officials decided to do so to lend the document more seriousness. Yet in the same press conference, Bartlett admitted that the attribution to the British arose out of a negotiation between an intelligence officer, Alan Foley, and an NSC staffer, Robert Joseph. As for the aluminum tubes, an anonymous senior administration official involved in vetting the speech explained that Bush used the word "suitable" with respect to the aluminum tubes because the claim had been called into question. David Barstow, William Broad, and Jeff Gerth, "Skewed Intelligence Data in March to War in Iraq," *The New York Times*, October 3, 2004.

**8.** Both Tyler Drumheller and a Defense Intelligence Agency detailee to the CIA, who was the only American ever to meet Curveball before the war, raised concerns about Powell's use of intelligence in the speech. Bob Drogin and Greg Miller, "'Curveball' Debacle Reignites Feud," *Los Angeles Times*, April 2, 2005; SSCI, 247ff. Analysts at the State Department's Bureau of Intelligence and Research (INR) objected to the discussion on the aluminum tubes, disputing Powell's claims that the tolerances of the tubes were higher than anything the U.S. would manufacture (SSCI, 430).

**9.** Scott Ritter, *Iraqi Confidential: The Untold Story of the Intelligence Conspiracy to Undermine the UN and Overthrow Saddam Hussein* (New York: Nation Books, 2005), 267-68.

**10.** SSCI, 248.

**11.** The SSCI report redacts most of the treatment of this defector. However, the one unredacted portion reads, "Committee staff asked a U.S. …polygraph expert…about the possibility of a 'false negative' resulting from a polygraph test." The discussion of a false negative suggests this defector failed a lie detector test.

**12.** David Rose, "Iraq's Arsenal of Terror," *Vanity Fair*, May 2002.

**13.** Commission on the Intelligence Capabilities of the United States Regarding Weapons of Mass Destruction, *Report to the President* (hereafter "Robb-Silberman Report"), March 31, 2005, 216 n 254. The report notes that "the NIE actually sourced its information to a *Vanity Fair* article, which quoted the INC source as an unnamed 'defector.'" SSCI, however, notes the "NIE described the source by name" (160).

**14.** Colum Lynch, "Chalabi Defends Intelligence on Arms," *The Washington Post,* June 11, 2003. The Senate Phase II report on the INC would hedge on whether Chalabi was responsible for the MBL claims. It does not consider Ritter's description of seeding the information with Chalabi. Senate Select Committee on Intelligence, *Report on the Use by the Intelligence Community of Information Provided by the Iraqi National Congress* (hereafter "Phase II INC"), September 8, 2006.

**15.** The most complete description of the Niger caper is in Carlo Bonini and Giuseppe d'Avanzo, "Berlusconi Behind Fake Yellowcake Dossier," *La Repubblica,* trans. Nur al-Cubicle, October 24, 2005, and updated November 14, 2005, at http://nuralcubicle.blogspot.com/2005/10/berlusconi-behind-fake-yellowcake.html. For excerpts of testimony from the Italians involved, see de Gondi's translation of the transcripts published by Gian Marco Chiocci and Mario Secchi in *Il Giornale* at European Tribune, 22 February 2006, http://www.eurotrib.com/story/2006/2/22/202646/733.

**16.** Take the first cable the CIA received from SISMI on October 15, 2001. That cable listed Nassirou Sabo as minister of foreign affairs involved in the uranium negotiations; Sabo was, in fact, the minister of foreign affairs on the date given. But the forged document on which that cable was based listed Allele El Hadj Habibou as foreign minister. He had served as foreign minister much earlier and appeared on letterhead dating to a former Nigerien regime. eRiposte, "Uranium from Africa and the Valerie Plame expose (Treasongate): A Synopsis," The Left Coaster, August 17, 2005, at http://www.theleftcoaster.com/archives/005211.php. Senators Pat Roberts, Kit Bond, and Orrin Hatch must be aware of this discrepancy, as they note in their "Additional View" in the SSCI that "the names and dates in the documents that the IAEA found to be incorrect were not names or dates included in the CIA reports" (SSCI, 444).

**17.** A footnote in the Robb-Silberman report reveals that one of the three Niger uranium reports includes information not found in the forgeries: "CIA/DO officials advised the Commission that in fact two of the reports were recalled and the third, which included information not included in the forged documents, was reissued with a caveat that the information the report contains may have been fabricated" (215 n 214). Elisabetta Burba, who provided a set of the forgeries to the U.S. in October 2002, never had the actual agreement. Burba, "Lo scoop che non c'era," *Panorama,* July 24, 2003, trans. Nur al-Cubicle, December 19, 2005, at http://nuralcubicle.blogspot.com/2005/12/panorama-magazine-niger-yellowcake.html. Yet the CIA reported getting a "verbatim text" of the accord on February 2002 (SSCI, 37). See also eRiposte, "Treasongate: The Niger Forgeries v. the CIA Intel Report—Part 7: The Case of the Fastidious Footnote," The Left Coaster, March 6, 2006, at http://www.theleftcoaster.com/archives/007022.php.

**18.** INR, "Niger-Iraq: Sale of Uranium to Iraq Unlikely," March 1, 2003.

**19.** SSCI, 56.

**20.** SSCI, 40-41.

**21.** *Comprehensive Report of the Special Advisor to the DCI* [hereafter "Duelfer Report"], September 30, 2004, volume 2, *Nuclear Weapons, 9.*

**22.** SSCI, 56.

**23.** Bob Woodward, *State of Denial: Bush at War, Part III* (New York: Simon & Schuster), 97.

**24.** SSCI, 55-57. Gerson is named as the other recipient of the memo in the press briefing where Hadley admitted receiving this warning (July 22, 2003).

**25.** SSCI, 58.

**26.** Barton Gellman and Dafna Linzer, "A 'Concerted Effort' to Discredit Bush Critic," *The Washington Post,* April 9, 2006.

**27.** SSCI, 88.

**28.** Michael Isikoff and David Corn were the first to reveal Turner's full name, in *Hubris: The Inside Story of Spin, Scandal, and the Selling of the Iraq War* (New York: Crown, 2006).

**29.** SSCI, 94.

**30.** SSCI, 103.

**31.** SSCI, 110.

**32.** David Albright, "Iraq's Aluminum Tubes: Separating Fact from Fiction," ISIS, December 5, 2003, 14; see http://www.isisonline.org/publications/iraq/IraqAluminumTubes12-5-03.pdf.

**33.** SSCI, 90.

**34.** Perhaps the skepticism among the task force is the reason James Woolsey, the former head of the CIA and a close ally of Cheney, repeatedly introduced INC defectors to the Defense Intelligence Agency, where their claims were treated with some credulity. The CIA "tends to not to talk to volunteers," Woolsey explained when asked why he bypassed the CIA (Phase II INC, 41).

**35.** SSCI, 260-63.

**36.** Woodward, *State of Denial,* 273.

**37.** However, this may be *another* instance in which Cheney prevented Bush from receiving certain kinds of intelligence. David Kay, the special advisor on Iraq's WMDs to CIA director George Tenet, says Bush, Condoleezza Rice, and

Colin Powell were not informed about the JITF's program. Kay believed news of the program had been deliberately withheld from these top officials (and from himself), though former deputy director of the CIA John McLaughlin dismisses that suspicion. Woodward, *State of Denial*, 273.

**38.** Isikoff and Corn reveal Valerie Wilson's role in the task force in *Hubris*.

**39.** Address to Conservative Political Action Committee, January 30, 2003; see http://www.whitehouse.gov/news/releases/2003/01/20030130-16.html.


**CHAPTER 2** DECONSTRUCTING JUDY


**40.** Judith Miller, "U.S. Officials Say Iraq Had Ability to Make Nuclear Weapon in 1981," *The New York Times*, June 9, 1981.

**41.** Franklin Foer, "The Source of the Trouble," *New York*, June 7, 2004.

**42.** Miller wrote of Mohammed Salah's interrogation in a 1993 story. On November 13, 2006, she was called to testify that, in her judgment, he had not been tortured. Since Patrick Fitzgerald tried this case, Salah's lawyers tried to impugn Miller by referencing her prewar reporting and her involvement in the CIA leak case. Salah's lawyer asked if her job was to cultivate special access to government officials, then print the stories they wanted. Jeff Coen, "Reporter Testifies in Hamas Case Trial," *Chicago Tribune*, November 14, 2006.

**43.** Rory O'Connor and William Scott Malone, "The 9/11 Story that Got Away," Alternet, May 18, 2006, at http://alternet.org/story/36388/. Richard Clarke, the former counterterrorism czar, has been a source for Miller in the past, and the tip came from the counterterrorism office, so it may been an attempt by Clarke or an associate to pressure the Bush administration to respond more aggressively to the chatter relating to Al Qaeda in the summer before 9/11.

**44.** Seth Mnookin describes Sulzberger's and Raines's protection of Miller in "Unreliable Sources," *Vanity Fair*, January 2006.

**45.** Ron Suskind describes the CIA response to the unvetted speech in *The One Percent Doctrine*, 168ff. Bob Woodward describes how Cheney used the speech without Bush's approval first. He made the speech in response to articles from Henry Kissinger, Brent Scowcroft, and James Baker opposing unilateral action. At the time, the administration had yet to settle on a policy. Bush's instructions to Cheney were simply, "Don't get me in trouble." Woodward, *Plan of Attack* (New York: Simon & Schuster, 2004), 164.

**46.** "Address to the VFW 103rd National Convention," August 26, 2002; see http://www.whitehouse.gov/news/releases/2002/08/20020826.html.

**47.** Elisabeth Bumiller, "Bush Aides Set Strategy to Sell Policy on Iraq," *The New York Times*, September 7, 2002.

**48.** Woodward, *State of Denial*, 147.

**49.** The "silver bullet" comment is from an interview with Ray Suarez on *The NewsHour with Jim Lehrer*, April 22, 2003. Miller had emphasized the importance of working with Iraqi scientists several weeks earlier, in an April 5 interview on CNN's *American Morning*. After Miller's "silver bullet" find, administration officials would increasingly cite the importance of scientists as well. For example, in a briefing on April 25, Donald Rumsfeld said, "There are people who in large measure have information that we need, and we need that information so that we can track down the weapons of mass destruction" (see http://www.defenselink.mil/transcripts/2003/tr20030425-secdef0126.html). So Miller's reporting appears to have paralleled a general DOD strategy for responding to the absence of WMD.

**50.** Judith Miller, "A Chronicle of Confusion in the U.S. Hunt for Hussein's Chemical and Germ Weapons," *The New York Times*, July 20, 2003.

**51.** Russ Baker, "'Scoops' and Truth at the *Times*," *The Nation*, June 23, 2003.

**52.** Duelfer Report, volume 3, *Chemical Warfare*, 49, 51.

**53.** Ibid., 49–53, 56.

**54.** Ibid., 53.

**55.** Phase II INC, 105–6.

**56.** Howard Kurtz, "Intra-*Times* Battle Over Iraqi Weapons," *The Washington Post*, May 26, 2003.

**57.** Miller's e-mail response to my questions, November 14, 2006.

**58.** Isikoff and Corn, *Hubris*, 220. Howard Kurtz reported a version of this letter in his "Embedded Reporter's Role in Army Unit's Actions Questioned by Military," *The Washington Post*, June 25, 2003.

**59.** Isikoff and Corn, *Hubris*, 220.

**60.** Ibid.

**61.** Kurtz, "Embedded Reporter's Role."

**62.** Kurtz, "Intra-*Times* Battle."

**63.** Ibid.

**64.** The accusation is one the INC continued to make. A May 12, 2003, article in *The New York Sun* cites "S.A.," a former Mukhabarat section chief in the employ of Chalabi, making allegations that Janabi had met with the Mukhabarat while in exile in the United States, Adam Daifallah, "Lively Politics Starts to Stir in Baghdad," *The New York Sun*, May 12, 2003. And the blog of an INC-connected researcher states directly that Janabi became a CIA asset in 2002; see Nibras Kazimi, "Another Colorful Janabi on Allawi's List," Talisman Gate, December 5, 2005, at http://talismangate.blogspot.com/2005/12/another-colorful-janabi-on-allawis.html.

**65.** Douglas Jehl and Dexter Filkins, "U.S. Moved to Undermine Iraqi Military Before War," *The New York Times,* August 10, 2003.

**66.** Kurtz, "Embedded Reporter's Role."

**67.** Miller explained in an e-mail response (November 14, 2006) to my questions that they found the document in "another section entirely, which was the original focus of the MET Alpha search." Which raises the question of why they brought MET Alpha's chaplain and Harold Rhode along to serve as experts on Jewish texts, as well as the question of when they got special permission from the commander of 75th XTF to use WMD teams to hunt down ancient scrolls.

**68.** Miller's colleague, Patrick Tyler, had reported the find a day earlier. "Opposition Groups to Help to Create Assembly in Iraq," *The New York Times,* May 6, 2003. Chalabi's group, the INC, maintained a contract with the Department of Defense as the continuation of the Iraq Collection Program. By having Chalabi's group collect the records of Saddam's regime, the DOD gave the collection an Iraqi face while immediately gaining access to the records of the regime. Chalabi, in turn, used the seized documents to issue threats against his political enemies.

**69.** Rhode accompanied Ahmed Chalabi as a DOD liaison. His role in the excursion is described in "Saddam's Secret Jewish Archives," *Moment,* October 13, 2003.

**70.** The document does appear in the Duelfer Report. The report translates the text of the document as follows:

> Enclosed is the report made by a friend from Uganda, Abdul Jamal Abdulnasser (Bika), about getting uranium and other important materials from his friend in Congo. He told us that he is ready to supply Iraq with these metals if Iraq wants them and it can be done without implicating Iraq. After we checked them, we told him we don't deal with these materials and we explained to him the circumstances of Iraq and the imposed sanctions, and that Iraq is not concerned about these matters right now. He said that he will do his best to help Iraq and Iraq's regime for Jihad together against our enemy, and he considers supporting the power of Iraq to be his participation which is the power for all Muslims, and he feels that his duties are to support and strengthen that power.

Curiously, the Duelfer Report obscures the provenance of the document, reporting that the ISG discovered the document, not the exploitation team, Miller's group. Duelfer Report, volume 2, *Nuclear Weapons,* 10-11.

**71.** Judith Miller, "U.S. Aides Say Iraqi Truck Could Be a Germ-War Lab," *The New York Times,* May 8, 2003.

**72.** CIA and DIA, *Iraqi Mobile Biological Warfare Agent Production Plants,* May 28, 2003. For McLaughlin's role, see Senate Select Committee on Intelligence, *Report of the Select Committee on Intelligence on Postwar Findings about Iraq's WMD Programs and Links to Terrorism and How They Compare with Prewar Assessments* (hereafter "Phase II WMD"), September 8, 2006, 35.

**73.** The article came at a time when *The New York Times* was under heavy pressure because of the Jayson Blair scandal, and Miller's reporting, in particular, had been called into question. Miller tried to return to Iraq to do further research on the MBLs, but she was not permitted to re-embed with the WMD hunters. As it happened, approving Miller's return trip to Iraq was one of Howell Raines and Gerard Boyd's last actions in the leadership of the paper, which brought in former executive editor Joseph Lelyveld on June 5. The pressure resulting from Jayson Blair—and possibly the return of Lelyveld—may explain why the June 7 article is much more balanced than the May 21 one. In the interim period, the *Times* came under a great deal of pressure to restore the credibility that had been damaged by Blair's and Miller's prewar and war reporting.

**74.** Phase II WMD.

**75.** In fact, it was precisely this timing, the re-release of the white paper the day before Bush's declaration, that the White House would appeal to in 2006 when trying to justify Bush's claim to have found mobile bioweapons labs:

> McCLELLAN: Well, first of all, as I held out a short time ago, the intelligence assessment was provided by the CIA and Defense Intelligence Agency on May 28, 2003. The President was asked a question on the very next day, and the President's statements were based on the joint assessment of the CIA and DIA that was publicly released the day before.

The question was prompted by a *Washington Post* article revealing the results of the Jefferson Project team (Joby Warrick, "Lacking Biolabs, Trailers Carried Case for War," April 12, 2006).

**CHAPTER 3** TRUTH AND CONSEQUENCES

**76.** Henry Waxman, the ranking Democrat on the House Government Reform Committee, proved particularly tenacious in investigating this story, sending inquiries to the White House on March 17, June 2, and June 10, 2003. Also, on March 14, Senator Jay Rockefeller had asked the FBI to investigate the Niger forgeries.

**77.** On June 15, the *Observer* newspaper announced an MI-6 (British intelligence) review had concluded the trailers could not be MBLs. "They are not mobile germ warfare laboratories. You could not use them for making biological weapons. They do not even look like them. They are exactly what the Iraqis said they were—facilities for the production of hydrogen gas to fill balloons." Peter Beaumont, Antony Barnett, and Gaby Hinsliff, "Iraqi Mobile Labs Nothing to Do with Germ Warfare, Report Finds," *The Observer,* June 15, 2003. Three days later, Ari Fleischer would insist the trailers were indeed mobile bioweapons labs:

> Mr. Fleischer: I think your characterization does not apply to the weapons labs which we know have no other purpose other than for the production of biological weapons.
>
> Q: So you're saying that there's no chance that they do produce hydrogen for weather balloons used in artillery?
>
> Mr. Fleischer: I think that theory is full of hot air.

Press Briefing, June 18, 2003. Later in the month, the State Department's intelligence service, INR, would refute the U.S. claims that the trailers were MBLs.

**78.** Joseph Wilson, "What I Didn't Find in Africa," *The New York Times,* July 6, 2003.

**79.** See, for example, Dana Priest and Karen DeYoung, "CIA Questioned Documents Linking Iraq, Uranium Ore," *The Washington Post,* March 22, 2003. Buried on page A30, the article would lay out many of the fissures that would explode when Wilson went public. It cites a White House spokesman saying all speeches are vetted, and a senior administration official saying the United States " will face significant problems in trying to find" WMDs. The article also reported the efforts by Senator Jay Rockefeller and Representative Henry Waxman to investigate the Niger claims.

**80.** Joseph Wilson, *The Politics of Truth,* 153.

**81.** SSCI, 39.

**82.** Ibid.

**83.** [Douglas Rohn,] "Notes—Niger/Iraq Uranium Meeting CIA," February 19, 2002. Available at http://www.nysun.com/pics/31062_1.php.

**84.** Isikoff and Corn's *Hubris* provides additional details on the role of Douglas Rohn in the February 19 meeting.

**85.** Ambassador Owens-Kirkpatrick met with the director of the French consortium in Niger in November 2001, and with the foreign minister in February 2002. Also in February, she and General Carlton Fulford met with Niger's president, Mamadou Tandja, and Foreign Minister Aichatou Mindaoudou. SSCI, 37, 40, 41–42.

**86.** Wilson describes the anecdote in *Politics of Truth,* 28–29.

**87.** SSCI, 43–46.

**88.** The reports officer explained to the SSCI that "he judged that the most important fact in the report was that the Nigerien officials admitted that the Iraqi delegation had traveled there in 1999." In a report on the interpretation of the report, the SSCI notes, "analysts did, however, find it interesting that the former Nigerien Prime Minister said an Iraqi delegation had visited Niger for what he believed was to discuss uranium sales". SSCI, 46.

**89.** SSCI, 46.

**90.** SSCI, 55.

**91.** See eRiposte, "Uranium from Africa: How 'Bought' Became 'Sought'— Introduction," The Left Coaster, May 1, 2006, at http://www.theleftcoaster.com/archives/007527.php.

**92.** "Hot and Cold Running Wilson Intelligence," *The Next Hurrah,* May 15, 2006, at http://thenexthurrah.typepad.com/the_next_hurrah/2006/05/hot_and_cold_ru.html; and eRiposte, "Uranium from Africa: The Wilson 'Workup' and the March 8, 2003 DIA Memo," The Left Coaster, May 8, 2006, at http://www.theleftcoaster.com/archives/007593.php.

**93.** Joseph Wilson, "How Saddam Thinks," *San Jose Mercury News,* October 13, 2002.

**94.** Wilson, *Politics of Truth,* 296-97.

**95.** Nicholas Kristof, "Missing in Action: Truth," *The New York Times,* May 6, 2003. After the SSCI appeared in July 2004, Wilson clarified what he had said to Kristof in the original interview, as he didn't remember claiming to have debunked—or even seen—the forgeries. Kristof reassured Wilson: "Don't worry. I remember you saying that you had not seen the documents. My recollection is that we had some information about the documents at that time—e.g. the names of people in them—but I do clearly remember saying that you had not been shown them." Wilson, *Politics of Truth,* lviii.

**96.** Walter Pincus, "CIA Did Not Share Doubt on Iraq Data," *The Washington Post,* June 12, 2003.

**97.** White House Press Gaggle, July 7, 2003.

**98.** White House Press Briefing (from Africa), July 10, 2003. Ironically, perhaps, Powell uses the discovery of the trailers—which State's own intelligence service had already concluded were designed for artillery balloons—as proof that the intelligence was well founded.

**99.** Press Gaggle, July 11, 2003. I first found this passage thanks to Todd Johnson, "Ari's Lies/Condi's Truth Telling: An Analysis," Daily Kos, July 27, 2005.

**100.** Ari Fleischer, on July 14, his last day as press secretary, would deny that Rice was referring to the SOTU when she discussed being forced to take Niger out. But that makes no sense given that Alan Foley testified to the same thing— that early drafts of the SOTU referenced Niger specifically. SSCI, 65. Furthermore, it would be nonsensical to confuse the Cincinnati speech with the SOTU, as Fleischer claimed, since the Niger claim was removed entirely from the Cincinnati speech, while only the reference to Niger and amounts were removed from the SOTU. Dana Milbank and Mike Allen make this point in "Iraq Flap Shakes Rice's Image," *The Washington Post*, July 27, 2003. Ron Suskind describes some of the pressure behind Rice's actions. On a morning (Tenet's time) phone call with Rice, he reminded her there was "a trail of paper, a few clear recollections, and visible actions." Suskind, *The One Percent Doctrine*, 244. The drafts of the SOTU are one of the items the White House refused to turn over to the SSCI for its Iraq report.

**101.** Statement by George Tenet, July 11, 2003. Available at http://www.cnn.com/2003/ALLPOLITICS/07/11/tenet.statement/.

**102.** "CIA Got Uranium Reference Cut in October," *The Washington Post*, July 13, 2003.

**103.** "Press Briefing on Iraq WMD and SOTU Speech," July 22, 2003. Hadley is still spinning with his comments here. The SSCI report (56) reveals the exact quote from this passage to read: "remove the sentence because the amount is in dispute and it is debatable whether it can be acquired from the source. We told Congress that the Brits have exaggerated this issue. Finally, the Iraqis already have 550 metric tons of uranium oxide in their inventory." Hadley effectively obscures the strong warning against the British intelligence, which was, after all, what the SOTU cited. In his discussion of further warnings, Hadley also omits the specific detail that the uranium would be unavailable from Niger based on the issues Wilson (and others) had raised, particularly the control over the uranium by the French consortium.

**104.** Wilson, *Politics of Truth*, 335.

**105.** The day after Tenet makes this statement, Fleischer picks up on the details about Ibrahim Mayaki, but botches the grammar of it, turning it (grammatically at least) into a tremendous attack.

> In fact, in one of the least known parts of this story, which is
> now, for the first time, public—and you find this in Director
> Tenet's statement last night—the official that—lower-level
> official sent from the CIA to Niger to look into whether or not

Saddam Hussein had sought yellowcake from Niger, Wilson, he—and Director Tenet's statement last night states the same former official, Wilson, also said that in June 1999 a business-man approached him and insisted that the former official, Wilson, meet an Iraqi delegation to discuss expanding commer-cial relations between Iraq and Niger. The former official inter-preted the overture as an attempt to discuss uranium sales.

This is in Wilson's report back to the CIA. Wilson's own report, the very man who was on television saying Niger denies it, who never said anything about forged documents, reports himself that officials in Niger said that Iraq was seeking to contact officials in Niger about sales.

Fleischer conflates whether it was Mayaki or Wilson who received the busi-nessman (Baghdad Bob) from Iraq: "Wilson…said that in June 1999 a business-man approached him and insisted that the former official, Wilson, meet an Iraqi delegation". Whether intentionally or accidentally, Fleischer suggests that Wilson coordinated with the Iraqi delegation.

**106.** John Dickerson, "Where Is My Subpoena?" Slate.com, February 7, 2006. Howard Fineman names Fleischer and Bartlett as the officials who prompted reporters to look into who sent Wilson. "Rove at War," *Newsweek,* July 17, 2005.

## CHAPTER 4 THE BELTWAY INSIDER

**107.** These two sentences reflect the column more generally, which shows the influence of two or three sharply competing agendas, which Novak didn't attempt to mediate.

**108.** Robert Novak, "Mission to Niger," July 14, 2003. Available at http://www.townhall.com/columnists/RobertDNovak/2003/07/14/mission_to_niger.

**109.** The call to declassify the report from Wilson's trip echoes a comment Rove made to Matt Cooper, saying new information would be declassified soon to provide insight into Wilson's trip.

**110.** Timothy Phelps and Knut Royce, "Columnist Blows CIA Agent's Cover," *Newsday,* July 22, 2003.

**111.** Mike Allen and Dana Priest, "Bush Administration Is Focus of Inquiry," *The Washington Post,* September 29, 2003.

**112.** The statute reads, "Whoever, having or having had authorized access to classified information that identifies a covert agent, intentionally discloses any information identifying such covert agent to any individual not authorized to receive classified information, knowing that the information disclosed so identifies such covert agent and that the United States is taking affirmative measures to conceal such covert agent's intelligence relationship to the United States, shall be fined under title 18 or imprisoned not more than ten years, or both." U.S. Code, Title 50, Section 421a.

**113.** Walter Pincus and Mike Allen, "Probe Focuses on Month Before Leak to Reporters," *The Washington Post,* October 12, 2003.

**114.** Murray Waas, "Rove-Novak Call Was Concern to Leak Investigators," *National Journal,* May 25, 2006.

**115.** James Moore and Wayne Slater, *The Architect* (New York: Crown, 2006), 255-56.

**116.** Robert Novak, "The CIA Leak," October 1, 2003. Available at Townhall.com.

**117.** According to Philip Taubman, who was Judith Miller's editor in fall 2003, she said something similar in response to his inquiry about whether she was involved in the leak. "'The answer was generally no,' Mr. Taubman said. Ms. Miller said the subject of Mr. Wilson and his wife had come up in casual conversation with government officials, Mr. Taubman said, but Ms. Miller said 'she had not been at the receiving end of a concerted effort, a deliberate organized effort to put out information.'" Don Van Natta, Adam Liptak, and Clifford Levy, "The Miller Case: A Notebook, a Cause, a Jail Cell and a Deal," *The New York Times,* October 16, 2003.

**118.** Fitzgerald does not include May on a the list of journalists known to have received a leak of Valerie Wilson's identity (which included Bob Woodward, Judith Miller, Bob Novak, Walter Pincus, and Matt Cooper), so the FBI must have determined this claim to be false during its investigation. Letter to Jeffress, Wells, and Tate, January 23, 2006.

**119.** In an August 1, 2005, column, Novak would again suggest it was possible to get the name "Plame" from *Who's Who,* again stopping short of claiming he did learn the name there: "Once it was determined that Wilson's wife suggested the mission, she could be identified as 'Valerie Plame' by reading her husband's entry in 'Who's Who in America.'" It was not until a July 2006 interview with Tim Russert that Novak first publicly stated unequivocally he did not get the name Plame until he read *Who's Who.*

> RUSSERT: Was that the very first time you had seen or heard the name, Valerie Plame?
>
> NOVAK: Yes.

RUSSERT: No one told you?

NOVAK: No.

*Meet the Press,* July 16, 2006.

**120.** Joshua Micah Marshall, http://www.talkingpointsmemo.com/archives/week_2003_10_05.php#002066, October 9, 2003.

**121.** Press Briefing, October 1, 2003.

**122.** Robert Novak, "The Wilsons for Gore," October 4, 2003. Available at Townhall.com.

**123.** Walter Pincus and Mike Allen, "Leak of Agent's Name Causes Exposure of CIA Front Firm," October 4, 2003. There's one more odd detail concerning Novak's reporting in fall 2003: A version of his October 1 column appeared later that week on the Human Events website using the name "Valerie Flame." See http://www.findarticles.com/p/articles/mi_qa3827/is_200310/ai_n9328212. While this may be a typo traceable to the syndication process, it's worth noting that Judith Miller was leaked the name "Valerie Flame" during her reporting on Wilson and his wife.

**124.** Novak also changed the attribution for the information related to the role of the Counterproliferation Division (CPD) in the trip. This is important because most insiders (like Novak, Armitage, and Scooter Libby) would understand that most CPD employees were classified, covered employees. The distinction is critical, then, because if someone told Novak that Mrs. Wilson worked in CPD, it would minimize the possibility that the person didn't know she was covert.

**125.** Nevertheless, in an interview and a column in 2006, Novak used the word "initiated" to describe his conversation with Rove. *Special Report with Brit Hume,* July 12, 2006. Robert Novak, "My Leak Case Testimony," July 13, 2006; available on Townhall.com.

**126.** *Special Report with Brit Hume,* July 12, 2006.

**127.** The conclusion that Valerie Wilson "suggested" Joe came in the "Additional Views" section of the SSCI, where senators recorded their views on which there was not consensus. It appears in an Additional View offered by senators Pat Roberts, Christopher Bond, and Orrin Hatch with the caveat "my Democrat [sic] colleagues refused to allow the following conclusions to appear in the report." Only three senators—not even a majority of the eight Republicans serving on the committee at the time—backed the conclusion. Yet Novak has, at various times, claimed that the "Additional Judgment" had no Democratic dissenters and had unanimous or Republican majority support. *Special Report with Brit Hume,* July 12, 2006; *Meet the Press,* July 16, 2006; Novak column, August 1, 2005.

**128.** Robert Novak, "Correcting the CIA," August 1, 2003. Available on Townhall.com.

**129.** Robert Novak, "Armitage's Leak," September 14, 2006. Available on Townhall.com.

**130.** *Washington Journal,* C-SPAN, September 15, 2006. My transcription.

**131.** Armitage's name had been leaked widely among the right-wing media in late 2005. Bloggers at The Next Hurrah then determined that Armitage's name was almost certainly the one redacted from a Fitzgerald filing in March 2006. See http://thenexthurrah.typepad.com/the_next_hurrah/2006/03/about_the_journ.html. His name was first confirmed in the wider media much later, with the publication of *Hubris.* Shortly after the publication of *Hubris,* Armitage did a long interview with CBS's David Martin explaining his involvement.

**132.** Interview with David Martin, CBS News, September 7, 2006. See also Warren Strobel, "Armitage Reveals That He Was a Source in Plame Leak," McClatchy News, September 7, 2006.

**133.** As Fitzgerald investigated further, he traced the source of Armitage's knowledge of Plame to a memo the State Department's intelligence service (INR) wrote. The memo referred to Valerie only as "a CIA WMD manager," not necessarily covert. The paragraph of the memo was marked S/NF (secret, no foreigners)— but that classification may well have related as much to the information on Wilson's trip, which the CIA had promised to keep confidential, as it did to Valerie. "INR Memo," available at http://www.nysun.com/pics/31062_1.php.

**134.** There is one problem with this explanation. There are two versions of the memo, both with cover distribution memos. The first, dated June 10, does not list Armitage as a recipient. Only the second one lists "D" (meaning Armitage, the deputy secretary of state). INR Memo, June 10, 2003, and July 7, 2003. See http://www.nysun.com/pics/31062_1.php and http://www.nysun.com/pics/31062_2_0.jpg.

**135.** The change to the memo is significant. The original memo notes that two key participants, Douglas Rohn and an INR nuclear analyst who had debunked the forgeries in October 2002, had been unavailable during the drafting of the memo. In the version printed out for Colin Powell, the memo removes the mention of the INR nuclear analyst. The difference is particularly curious given that the INR memo doesn't include the first e-mail the analyst wrote debunking the forgeries, including only e-mails from January 2003. In other words, the INR memo hides how soon the State Department had debunked the forgeries for a memo to Colin Powell, removed all mention of the person who had done that debunking.

**136.** Interview with David Martin, CBS News, September 7, 2006.

**137.** Michael Duffy, "Leaking with a Vengeance," *Time,* October 5, 2003.

**138.** "Press Availability," October 7, 2003.

## CHAPTER 5 BEAT THE PRESS

**139.** For example, Attorney General John Ashcroft had paid Karl Rove hundreds of thousands of dollars over the years for political consulting, and Rove was the most prominent suspect in the leak in fall 2003. And acting Deputy Attorney General Robert McCallum, who was involved in the reporting structure to Ashcroft, was one of President Bush's good friends from Yale; they had belonged to the same secret society.

**140.** Eric Lichtblau, "Ashcroft Briefed Regularly on Inquiry into C.I.A. Leak," *The New York Times,* October 22, 2003.

**141.** At first, the appointment seemed to be another case of influence; Comey and Fitzgerald are very close friends, and Fitzgerald is godparent to one of Comey's children. But in this matter, as in others (such as the NSA domestic surveillance program), Comey has shown a remarkable degree of independence relating to the administration's activities.

**142.** Paul Harris, "St. Patrick's Day," *The Observer,* February 12, 2006.

**143.** "The investigation concerned any government officials who leaked the identity of Valerie Plame to any reporters, not just Robert Novak, and...the investigation was not limited to determining whether violations of [the IIPA] statute had occurred." Government's Reply in Support of Its Motion to Preclude Evidence, Comment, and Argument Regarding the Government's Charging Decisions, November 17, 2006.

**144.** Fitzgerald also had to pursue the leak to Knut Royce and Tim Phelps of *Newsday,* who had received confirmation of Wilson's covert status for an article published July 22. He initiated discussions with them to testify, but then dropped it. Presumably, Fitzgerald figured out who had confirmed that information to them—and determined that their source had not violated the IIPA law.

**145.** Matthew Cooper, Massimo Calabresi, and John Dickerson, "A War on Wilson?" *Time,* July 17, 2003.

**146.** In fact, he did not have all relevant e-mails. He appears to have been missing an e-mail from Karl Rove to Stephen Hadley recording a conversation with Cooper. And as Fitzgerald revealed in a January letter to Libby's lawyers, not all 2003 e-mails were "preserved through the normal archiving process." Letter to Libby's lawyers, January 23, 2006.

**147.** Indictment, *United States of America v. I. Lewis Libby,* October 28, 2005, 18-19.

**148.** Fitzgerald mentions a third reporter whom Libby claims to have told of Plame's identity in his August 27, 2004, affidavit. Bloggers have determined the third reporter is probably Kessler based on incomplete redactions (see the stem in the redaction in paragraph 3 on page 3), spacing, and the timing of his known discussions with journalists.

**149.** Indictment.

**150.** Libby is notorious for taking detailed but almost completely illegible notes of meetings and his other daily activities. During the first few months of the investigation, the FBI got his notes and interpreted them (it's not clear how).

**151.** Scooter Libby, at least, was first asked to sign a waiver at his second FBI interview, on November 26, 2003. He did not sign one, however, until January 5, 2004, after Fitzgerald renewed the call for administration officials to sign waivers. I. Lewis Libby's Motion In Limine to Exclude Evidence Relating to Reporters' First Amendment Litigation, Contempt Proceedings, and Judith Miller's Incarceration, October 30, 2006, 3.

**152.** The limited exception is Matt Cooper. After Cooper testified about his conversation with Libby, Fitzgerald subpoenaed him a second time, looking for information on any sources who discussed Wilson with him. Yet, as it happened, Fitzgerald learned of Cooper's source before he testified. Just days after Cooper's attempt to quash the subpoena was denied, Rove admitted he might have talked to Cooper. Then, before Cooper arranged a waiver with Rove, *Time* released internal e-mails revealing Rove as Cooper's source. So as it happened, even Cooper did not have to reveal his source.

**153.** Robert Novak, "My Leak Case Testimony," July 12, 2006.

**154.** Matt Cooper, "What Scooter Libby and I Talked About," *Time,* November 7, 2005.

**155.** As it turns out, Cooper's testimony was equally damaging for Libby, as the discrepancy between Cooper's version and Libby's version of the story netted Libby a perjury charge. Indictment 20-22.

**156.** Cooper, "What Scooter Libby."

**157.** Carol D. Leonnig and Jim VandeHei, "Testimony by Rove and Libby Examined," *The Washington Post,* July 23, 2005.

**158.** Libby perceived Matthews's reporting to be a personal attack and even insinuated he was an anti-Semite for his reporting. Mickey Kaus was one of the first to report the anti-Semite accusation in "The Hole in the 'Oil Spot' Strategy," November 14, 2005, at http://www.slate.com/id/2129634/&#mystery2.

**159.** Motion of Non-Party Tim Russert to Quash Grand Jury Subpoena. June 4, 2004.

**160.** *Special Report with Brit Hume,* July 12, 2006.

**161.** Miller claims to have pitched a story on the Wilsons to her editors, and she has admitted to speaking to other sources on the topic:

> Mr. Fitzgerald asked if I could recall discussing the Wilson–Plame connection with other sources. I said I had, though I could not recall any by name or when those conversations occurred....Mr. Fitzgerald asked whether I ever pursued an article about Mr. Wilson and his wife. I told him I had not, though I considered her connection to the C.I.A. potentially newsworthy. I testified that I recalled recommending to editors that we pursue a story.

But *The New York Times* denies that Miller tried to publish the story—kind of. It says only that Miller never asked Jill Abramson to write an article:

> Ms. Miller said in an interview that she "made a strong recommendation to my editor" that an article be pursued. "I was told no," she said. She would not identify the editor. Ms. Abramson, the Washington bureau chief at the time, said Ms. Miller never made any such recommendation.

The nondenial denial is curious for another reason: The *Times* has consistently hidden the role of Joseph Lelyveld in the leak period. Lelyveld served as acting executive editor from June 5 to July 30, the entire period of the leak. Yet the *Times* uses constructions like "On July 30, 2003, Mr. Keller became executive editor after his predecessor, Howell Raines," which hide the entire transition from Raines to Lelyveld to Keller. The *Times's* dishonesty about Lelyveld suggests there's reason to doubt their version of Miller's negotiations with her editors. Miller, "My Four Hours Testifying Before the Grand Jury," and Van Natta et al., "The Miller Case," both published in *The New York Times* on October 16, 2005.

**162.** Libby actually spoke to Miller three times during the week of July 7— at a two-hour meeting at the St. Regis Hotel on July 8, in a short phone call while Miller was in a cab on July 12, then in a longer call after she had reached her home on Long Island. Fitzgerald doesn't mention the second conversation on July 12 in his August 2004 affidavit, so he may have learned of the third conversation after that point. August 27, 2004, Affidavit of Patrick Fitzgerald.

**163.** Van Natta et al., "The Miller Case."

**164.** Ibid.

**165.** And this is just the part of the story *The New York Times* allowed to be told. Apparently, the reporters working on the story were prohibited from talking to Russ Lewis, then CEO and president of the Times Company, who had taken a lead in strategizing a response to the Miller case. When asked why he wouldn't let them speak to Lewis, Sulzberger said, "Because I don't know what the fuck he's going to tell you." Seth Mnookin, "Unreliable Source," *Vanity Fair*, January 2006.

**166.** Miller quoted weapons expert Amy Smithson doubting that WMDs would be found in Iraq. Judith Miller and Doug Jehl, "US Forces Have Searched Few Weapons Sites," *The New York Times*, April 5, 2003. The paper issued the following correction to the article, explaining what Miller did:

> In fact the comments were paraphrases of a remark Ms. Smithson made in an e-mail exchange for The Times's background information, on the condition that she would not be quoted by name. Attempts to reach her before publication were unsuccessful. Thus the comments should not have been treated as quotations or attributed to her.

**167.** The op-ed brought up another issue, the fact that Fitzgerald and Miller had tussled before. Fitzgerald had in 2004 confronted Miller in a different case, a terrorism investigation, in which by making press inquiries, she had tipped off an Islamic charity named the Holy Land Fund of an imminent raid. Someone in government had leaked the information to Miller, and twice she had passed that on (with the second charity, the Global Relief Foundation, she passed the tip on to another *New York Times* reporter, who called the charity), giving the charities warning of the raids. Fitzgerald needed the call data, he argued, to help determine whether the leak was a deliberate attempt to warn the charities of the raids. On February 24, 2005, Fitzgerald had had his attempt denied to get Miller's call data to discover her source (though in August 2006 a circuit court reversed this decision and a November 27, 2006, Supreme Court ruling finally gave Fitzgerald access to the data). The involvement of Fitzgerald and Miller in both cases made it seem as if the prosecutor had a personal issue with Miller, making Miller's July 2005 imprisonment all the more shocking.

**168.** Walter Pincus, "Anonymous Sources: Their Use in a Time of Prosecutorial Interest," *Nieman Watchdog*, July 6, 2005.

**169.** For example, Fitzgerald would learn, after Libby's indictment, that Richard Armitage had leaked to Bob Woodward on June 13. Since Woodward didn't publish the story, Fitzgerald didn't know to ask about it.

**170.** For example, Fitzgerald did not originally subpoena Judith Miller's June 23 conversation with Libby.

**171.** For example, both Bob Woodward and Bob Novak came to Richard Armitage with still-classified information, which they used to preface their questions that elicited information about Valerie Wilson's identity. Woodward offered up that he knew that Joe Wilson was the envoy described in Pincus's story. And Novak introduced his question to Armitage by saying that Joe Wilson had never worked at the CIA. While Pincus (or someone else at the *Post*) is a possible source for Joe Wilson's role, it's not clear where Novak would have learned affirmatively that Joe Wilson had never worked at the CIA.

**172.** Joseph Wilson, "On Judith Miller's Sentencing," July 6, 2005, at http://www.tpmcafe.com/story/2005/7/6/15588/40407.

## CHAPTER 6 THE SPIN DOCTOR

**173.** Wilson, *Politics of Truth,* 372.

**174.** Press Briefing, September 29, 2003.

**175.** McClellan noted, "If you have any specific information to bring to my attention—like I said, there has been nothing that's been brought to our attention." Libby appealed to Cheney to have McClellan make the following statement:

> People have made too much of the difference in
> How I described Karl and Libby
> I've talked to Libby.
> I said it was ridiculous about Karl
> And it is ridiculous about Libby.
> Libby was not the source of the Novak story.
> And he did not leak classified information.

Government's Response to Third Motion to Compel Discovery, April 5, 2006. Note that Libby was parsing here, denying any connection to the Novak story, but not denying leaking.

**176.** Richard Leiby, "The Liberal on Karl Rove's Case," *The Washington Post,* December 7, 2005.

**177.** For example, at a time when Rove was a subject of the investigation, Luskin insisted Rove was not a target, while not admitting Fitzgerald's concerted focus on his client's role in the case. And just days before Matt Cooper would have to go to jail for protecting Rove, Luskin claimed, "If Matt Cooper is going to jail to protect a source, it's not Karl he's protecting."

**178.** Michael Duffy and Timothy J. Burger, "NOC NOC, Who's There: A Special Kind of Agent," *Time,* October 27, 2003. Viveca Novak contributed to this article, so she may have been the source for the detail that Rove had been interviewed by the FBI.

**179.** Cooper would receive this, his second subpoena, on September 13, 2004. It was written more generally than his first one, seeking "any and all documents… [relating to] conversations between Matthew Cooper and official source(s) prior to July 14, 2003, concerning in any way: former Ambassador Joseph Wilson; the 2002 trip by former Ambassador Wilson to Niger; Valerie Wilson Plame, a/k/a Valerie Wilson, a/k/a Valerie Plame (the wife of former Ambassador Wilson); and/or any affiliation between Valerie Wilson Plame and the CIA." Appeals Court Opinion, "In Re: Grand Jury Subpoena Judith Miller," reissued February 3, 2006.

**180.** *The McLaughlin Group,* July 1, 2005.

**181.** Michael Isikoff, "The Rove Factor?," *Newsweek,* July 11, 2005; Carol Leonnig, "Lawyer Says Rove Talked to Reporter, Did Not Leak Name," *The Washington Post,* July 3, 2005.

**182.** Byron York, "Lawyer: Cooper 'Burned' Karl Rove," National Review Online, July 12, 2005.

**183.** Joe Hagan, "US Prosecutor Says Journalists Deserve Jail," *The Wall Street Journal,* July 6, 2005. In the article Luskin also is described as explaining that Rove didn't ask anyone to treat him as a confidential source in the CIA leak—this, just days after Michael Isikoff had read him the content of Cooper's e-mail, joking about Rove putting him on "double super secret background." *Hubris,* 273, 388.

**184.** *Hardball with Chris Matthews,* October 12, 2005.

**185.** Matt Cooper, "What I Told the Grand Jury," *Time,* July 25, 2005.

**186.** "Press Conference with Prime Minister Singh," July 18, 2005.

**187.** The *Times* may not have been the first with the scoop. On July 12, Murray Waas told Luskin he was preparing to write about Rove's involvement, but Luskin asked him to wait a few days. "I spoke to Luskin and told him that I was preparing a lengthier story detailing Rove's contacts with Novak and others. Luskin asked me to delay publication for a day or two, before deciding on what he wanted to say for the article. He said he would comment for the record regarding what he understood transpired between Rove and Novak." Rather than have Waas report Rove's involvement first, the *Times* reported a version much friendlier to Rove. American Prospect Online, July 15, 2005.

**188.** Thomas DeFrank and Kenneth Bazinet, "Prez Ex-Flack Lumped with Rove?" New York *Daily News,* July 15, 2005.

**189.** Richard Stevenson, "State Dept. Memo Gets Scrutiny in Leak Inquiry on CIA Officer," *The New York Times,* July 16, 2005; Mike Allen and Jim VandeHei,

"Memo Is a Focus of CIA Leak Probe," *The Washington Post*, July 16, 2005; Richard Keil and William Roberts, "Special Prosecutor's Probe Centers on Rove, Memo, Phone Calls," Bloomberg, July 18, 2005; Anne Marie Squeo and John D. McKinnon, "Memo Underscored Issue of Shielding Plame's Identity," *The Wall Street Journal*, July 19, 2005; Walter Pincus and Jim VandeHei, "Plame's Name Marked as Secret," *The New York Times*, July 21, 2005. Two articles appear to be State Department pushback against published discussions of the memo: Tom Hamburger, "Memo May Hold Key to CIA Leak," *Los Angeles Times*, July 17, 2005, and Barry Schweid, "Memo Gets Attention in Probe of CIA Leak," Associated Press, July 20, 2005. And just one article quotes from an Ari Fleischer surrogate: "Fleischer told the grand jury that he never saw the memo, a person familiar with the testimony said, speaking on condition of anonymity....Fleischer has told the grand jury that he did not return Novak's call, a person familiar with the testimony said." David Johnston, Douglas Jehl, and Richard W. Stevenson, "For Bush Aides in CIA Case, 2nd Issue Arises," *The New York Times*, July 23, 2005.

**190.** Richard Keil and William Roberts, "Special Prosecutor's Probe Centers on Rove, Memo, Phone Calls," Bloomberg, July 18, 2005.

**191.** David Johnston, Douglas Jehl, and Richard W. Stevenson, "For Bush Aides in CIA Case, 2nd Issue Arises," *The New York Times*, July 23, 2005.

**192.** Richard Stevenson, "State Dept. Memo Gets Scrutiny in Leak Inquiry on CIA Officer," *The New York Times*, July 16, 2005, and Tom Hamburger, "Memo May Hold Key to CIA Leak," *Los Angeles Times*, July 17, 2005.

**193.** Tom Hamburger, "Memo May Hold Key to CIA Leak," *Los Angeles Times*, July 17, 2005; Walter Pincus and Jim VandeHei, "Plame's Name Marked as Secret," *The New York Times*, July 21, 2005.

**194.** Michael Isikoff, "CIA Leak Probe: Powell's Grand Jury Appearance," *Newsweek* August 9, 2004.

**195.** VandeHei and Carol Leonnig, "Rove Told Jury Libby May Have Been His Source In Leak Case," *The Washington Post*, October 20, 2005.

**196.** Appeals Court Opinion, "In Re: Grand Jury Subpoena Judith Miller," reissued February 3, 2006.

**197.** Walter Pincus and Jim VandeHei, "Plame's Name Marked as Secret," *The New York Times*, July 21, 2005.

**198.** This is precisely what Libby's lawyers would do after he was indicted—point to this flurry of leaks as potential evidence that Fleischer had cooperated with Fitzgerald because he himself was implicated in the leak:

> The press has reported that Mr. Fleischer reviewed the State Department report sent to Air Force One during the Africa trip, and has speculated that he divulged information to reporters

concerning Ms. Wilson during the trip. (A Leak, Then a Deluge, Exhibit I; Prosecutor's Probe Centers on Rove, Memo, Phone Calls (Update 2), Bloomberg, July 18, 2003, attached as Exhibit J.) On cross-examination at trial, the defense will be entitled to question Mr. Fleischer on issues such as: (1) when and how he learned about Ms. Wilson's identity; (2) the nature of his conversations with reporters; and (3) any efforts he undertook to criticize Mr. Wilson. If the press reports are correct, and Mr. Fleischer disclosed information concerning Ms. Wilson to reporters, he himself may have been a subject of Mr. Fitzgerald's investigation. Mr. Fleischer may thus have a motive to shade his testimony. Such possible bias will be vigorously explored on cross-examination.

Third Motion of I. Lewis Libby to Compel Discovery under Rule 16 and Brady, March 17, 2006.

**199.** Viveca Novak and Mike Allen, "A Contingency Plan," *Time,* October 17, 2005 (October 24, 2005, issue).

**200.** *Larry King Live,* October 27, 2005.

**201.** There's a bit of a dance here, of course. If someone under suspicion—Libby or Rove—raised Armitage's name directly, it would suggest they had compared notes with someone about the case, either within the administration or Novak or Woodward, and learned that Armitage was Novak's first source. They needed to find a way to bring it out indirectly. And using the press to force these issues at a convenient time was an effective means of doing so.

**202.** Fitzgerald stated, "In fact, Mr. Libby was the first official known to have told a reporter when he talked to Judith Miller in June of 2003 about Valerie Wilson." Press Conference, October 28, 2005. This made Woodward realize Fitzgerald didn't know about their conversation. A few days later, Woodward persuaded Armitage to admit to their conversation. Bob Woodward, "Testifying in the CIA Leak Case," *The Washington Post,* November 16, 2005.

**203.** It's unclear how Woodward knew, before he met with Armitage, Joe Wilson's identity as the still-unnamed envoy to Niger. Perhaps Woodward figured it out based on his own reporting; perhaps he learned it internally at *The Washington Post;* perhaps he learned it from someone at the Office of the Vice President while working on his book *Bush at War.* It is worth noting, however, that both Woodward and Bob Novak came to their meetings with Richard Armitage having learned classified information they used to goad Armitage into sharing further details of the trip to Niger.

**204.** Woodward, "Testifying in the CIA Leak Case."

**205.** There is a dispute about this. Woodward claims to have twice asked Armitage to release him to tell about the conversation, which presumably would have served to remind Armitage of the conversation. "Woodward said he had tried twice before, once in 2004 and once earlier this year, to persuade the source to remove the confidentiality restriction, but with no success." Viveca Novak, "Why Woodward's Source Came Clean," *Time*, November 18, 2005. But Armitage claims he had totally forgotten about the conversation until Woodward reminded him of it in November 2005. "He said he hadn't recalled that conversation until Woodward reminded him of it later, and he then immediately called the FBI and sought another meeting with Fitzgerald." Interview with David Martin, CBS News, September 7, 2006.

**206.** The e-mail was actually leaked just before Cooper testified in July 2005. This raised the specter of witness tampering: Cooper didn't remember calling Rove about welfare reform, so it seemed as though the leak may have been designed to coach Cooper's testimony regarding the reason he called Rove.

**207.** John Solomon, "Rove E-Mailed Security Officer About Talk," Associated Press, July 16, 2005.

**208.** Isikoff and Corn, *Hubris*, 401.

**209.** Fitzgerald first subpoenaed records relating to Cooper on January 22, 2004.

**210.** The critical Novak-Luskin conversation has been variously claimed to have occurred in October 2003 and January, March, and May 2004. None of these dates, however, account for all the discrepancies of the story. Either Luskin printed out the e-mail of his own accord and then referred back to it after he learned that reporters at *Time* considered Rove to be Cooper's source, yet still waited at least five months to bring the e-mail to Fitzgerald; or his conversation explains why he printed out the e-mail, but leaves almost a year's delay before he handed the e-mail over to Fitzgerald.

**211.** The articles on the CIA leak to which Viveca Novak contributed during the period of interest are: "Leaking with a Vengeance," October 5, 2003; "Why Leakers Rarely Do Time," October 13, 2003; "NOC NOC, Who's There," October 27, 2003; "A Shifting Probe," January 12, 2004. March 1, 2004, and May 2004 included no reporting on the CIA leak. Viveca Novak, "What Viveca Novak Told Fitzgerald," *Time*, December 11, 2005. Those identified meetings all coincide with important Rove activities: October 2003 (after the announcement of the investigation), January 2004 (after the request that administration officials sign waivers, but almost certainly before records of conversations with Cooper were subpoenaed), March 2004 (after Rove testified the first and second times), May 2004 (after Cooper was subpoenaed).

212. Her biggest scoops on Rove were the hints about Mr. X's identity and, presumably based on those hints, an important story about why Armitage came forward to testify. Viveca Novak, "Why Woodward's Source Came Clean," *Time*, November 18, 2005.

213. Viveca Novak, "What Viveca Novak Told Fitzgerald," *Time*, December 11, 2005.

214. Novak offered a slightly different version, saying that Rove responded, "Oh, you know that too?" *Special Report with Brit Hume*, July 12, 2006.

215. Libby Indictment, 8.

216. Isikoff and Corn, *Hubris*, 297.

217. Broder claims Rove simply confirmed Valerie Wilson's identity, rather than offering it up as Cooper's first source. He implies Wilson claimed to have written a memo debunking the Niger case, when Wilson made clear in the op-ed that he did not write the report on the trip himself. And Broder concludes, "In fact, the prosecutor concluded that there was no crime; hence, no indictment," when in fact we don't know why Fitzgerald did not indict Rove.

218. David Broder, "One Leak and a Flood of Silliness," *The Washington Post*, September 7, 2006.


## CHAPTER 7  THE FALL GUY

219. Lewis Libby, *The Apprentice* (New York: Thomas Dunne Books), 2001.

220. Bob Woodward tells an interesting anecdote in *Plan of Attack*. Shortly after 9/11, a *New York Times* article depicted Libby and Wolfowitz as advocating a much harder-line response, including against Iraq, than Powell. Libby complained to Richard Armitage, "I didn't like to see my name next to [Powell's name]" (50).

221. Patrick Tyler, "US Strategy Plan Calls for Insuring No Rival Develops," *The New York Times*, March 8, 1992.

222. James Mann, *Rise of the Vulcans*, 210.

223. Ibid., 209–13.

224. An example is the way Cheney repeatedly inserted John Bolton in the multiparty negotiations with North Korea (and attempted to have him replace James Kelly as the lead negotiator in multiparty talks). In his testimony on Bolton's appointment to be UN ambassador, Ambassador Thomas Hubbard described several instances of ways that Bolton's words and deeds thwarted the administration's stated policy of negotiations. Interview of Ambassador Thomas Hubbard with Regard to the Bolton Nomination, Senate Committee on Foreign Relations, April 28, 2005.

**225.** Robert Dreyfuss, "Vice Squad," American Prospect Online, May 8, 2006.

**226.** Libby worked closely with John Hannah, David Wurmser, and Bill Luti on such propaganda efforts.

**227.** Murray Waas, "The Meeting," *The American Prospect,* August 6, 2005; John Conyers, Letter to I. Lewis Libby, August 8, 2005.

**228.** Patrick Fitzgerald, Letter to Joseph Tate, September 12, 2005.

**229.** Scooter Libby, Letter to Judith Miller, September 15, 2005.

**230.** Judith Miller, "My Four Hours Testifying in the Federal Grand Jury Room," *The New York Times,* October 16, 2005. In August 2003, Miller presented a paper on WMD counterproliferation at a conference titled "In Search of an American Grand Strategy for a New Middle East" in Aspen, as part of the Aspen Institute's Aspen Strategy Group. It should be noted that Vice President Dick Cheney has a home in Jackson Hole, and Scooter Libby was known to travel there with Cheney frequently.

**231.** My e-mail exchange with Miller, November 14, 2006.

**232.** Susan Schmidt and Jim VandeHei, "N.Y. Times Reporter Released from Jail," *The Washington Post,* September 30, 2005. Miller's colleagues at *The New York Times* also published an account from "someone...briefed on" Libby's testimony.

> According to someone who has been briefed on Mr. Libby's testimony and who believes that his statements show he did nothing wrong, Ms. Miller asked Mr. Libby during their conversations in July 2003 whether he knew Joseph C. Wilson IV, the former ambassador who wrote an Op-Ed article in The Times on July 6, 2003, criticizing the Bush administration. Ms. Miller's lawyers declined to discuss the conversations.

> Mr. Libby said that he did not know Mr. Wilson but that he had heard from the C.I.A. that the former ambassador's wife, an agency employee, might have had a role in arranging a trip that Mr. Wilson took to Africa on behalf of the agency to investigate reports of Iraq's efforts to obtain nuclear material. Mr. Wilson's wife is Ms. Wilson.

> Mr. Libby did not know her name or her position at the agency and therefore did not discuss these matters with Ms. Miller, the person who had been briefed on the matter said. Ms. Miller said she believed that the agreement between her lawyers and Mr. Fitzgerald "satisfies my obligation as a reporter to keep faith with my sources."

David Johnston and Doug Jehl, "Times Reporter Free from Jail; She Will Testify," *The New York Times*, September 30, 2005. Murray Waas reported that at least three news outlets received this leak, though two declined to publish it because the source had a "strong bias on behalf of Libby." "CIA Leak Prosecutor Focuses on Libby," *National Journal*, October 18, 2005.

**233.** Miller's subpoena requested information on meetings "occurring from on or about July 6, 2003, to on or about July 13, 2003." Appeals Court Opinion, "In Re: Grand Jury Subpoena Judith Miller," reissued February 3, 2006. Fitzgerald did get testimony from at least one journalist regarding an earlier conversation; Walter Pincus testified about his conversation with Libby leading up to his June 12, 2003, article. In addition, Bob Novak was subpoenaed about a conversation with Scooter Libby. The date and subject of that meeting have not been explained.

**234.** David Johnston and Richard Stevenson, "Times Reporter Gives Testimony in CIA Leak Case," *The New York Times*, October 1, 2005.

**235.** As the indictment laid out, the central questions of the investigation had to do with:

> When and how Libby learned that Valerie Wilson worked at the CIA

> Whether and when Libby revealed Valerie Wilson's CIA affiliation to members of the media

> The language Libby used when disclosing information to the media

> Whether Libby knew the information he disclosed was classified at the time he disclosed it

> Whether Libby was truthful with the FBI and grand jury investigating the leak

**236.** Government's Memorandum in Opposition to Defendant's Motion to Preclude Evidence and Argument Relating to Valerie Wilson's Employment Status. November 14, 2006.

**237.** Press Briefing, October 28, 2005.

**238.** "The Kristof article caused inquiry to be made within the OVP, and eventually by the defendant, about Mr. Wilson's trip, and this led to relevant conversations between the defendant and other witnesses...during which the defendant was advised of the CIA employment of Mr. Wilson's wife." Government

Response to Court Inquiry Regarding News Articles the Government Intends to Offer as Evidence During Trial, May 12, 2006.

**239.** The indictment describes the documents as lacking Wilson's name— Libby and another OVP employee wrote Wilson's name at the top of the report. As the SSCI reports, the CIA report on Wilson's trip didn't name Wilson: "The report did not identify the former ambassador by name or as a former ambassador, but described him as 'a contact with excellent access who does not have an established reporting record.'"

**240.** Appeals Court Opinion, "In Re: Grand Jury Subpoena Judith Miller," reissued February 3, 2006.

**241.** For example, the chairman of the fund, Mel Sembler, served as ambassador to Italy at the time when Italian intelligence, SISMI, was laundering the information in the Niger forgeries and cabling it to the CIA. Similarly, former director of the CIA James Woolsey introduced several of the INC-sponsored fabricators to U.S. intelligence in the lead-up to the Iraq War. Both men, then, played key roles in the deceptions that led to war.

**242.** Copy of op-ed submitted into evidence, May 12, 2006. See also Government Response, May 12, 2006.

**243.** Walter Pincus, "Anonymous Sources: Their Use in a Time of Prosecutorial Interest," *Nieman Watchdog,* July 6, 2005.

**244.** Scooter Libby Grand Jury Testimony, March 24, 2004. Submitted as evidence May 24, 2006.

**245.** Letter to Scooter Libby's Lawyers, January 23, 2006; Hearing Transcript, May 5, 2006.

**246.** Hearing Transcript, May 5, 2006.

**247.** Bob Woodward, "Testifying in the CIA Leak Case," *The Washington Post,* November 16, 2005. In "A 'Concerted Effort' to Discredit Bush Critic," Barton Gellman and Dafna Linzer report that Libby used the word "vigorous" with Woodward, the same word he is reported to have used with Miller. *The Washington Post,* April 9, 2006.

**248.** Government's Memorandum in Opposition to Defendant's Motion to Preclude Evidence and Argument Relating to Valerie Wilson's Employment Status. November 14, 2006.

**249.** "Yellowcake Remix," *The Wall Street Journal,* July 17, 2004.

**250.** Government's Response to Defendant's Third Motion to Compel Discovery, April 5, 2006.

**251.** Government's Memorandum in Opposition to Defendant's Motion to Preclude Evidence and Argument Relating to Valerie Wilson's Employment Status, November 14, 2006.

**252.** Government's Response to Defendant's Third Motion to Compel Discovery, April 5, 2006.

**253.** As we have seen, Miller was also leaked the still-classified white paper briefing on the mobile bioweapons labs (MBLs) just two months earlier, for her May 21 article.

**254.** Government's Memorandum in Opposition to Defendant's Motion to Preclude Evidence and Argument Relating to Valerie Wilson's Employment Status, November 14, 2006.

**255.** Ibid.

**256.** *Meet the Press,* September 10, 2006.

**Marcy Wheeler** blogs under the name "emptywheel" at the political blog The Next Hurrah. Her PhD and academic background—relating to citizen journalism at times of heavy propaganda—brings a unique perspective to her blogging and the CIA leak case. Several of her posts have scooped the mainstream media's coverage of the Plame Affair, including her coverage of Scooter Libby's NIE leaks. She is a self-employed business consultant based in Ann Arbor, MI.